Better Homes and Gardens®

step-by-step
garden basics

Better Homes and Gardens® Books
Des Moines, Iowa

Better Homes and Gardens® Books
An imprint of Meredith® Books

Step-By-Step Garden Basics
Writer: Liz Ball
Project Editor: David Haupert
Art Director: Lyne Neymeyer
Creative Consultant: Karen Weir-Jimerson
Copy Chief: Catherine Hamrick
Copy and Production Editor: Terri Fredrickson
Contributing Copy Editor: Barbara Feller Roth
Contributing Proofreaders: Mary Duerson, Sue Fetters, Mary Pas
Contributing Photographers: Derek Fell, Saba S. Tien
Indexer: Colleen Johnson
Electronic Production Coordinator: Paula Forest
Editorial and Design Assistants: Kaye Chabot, Mary Lee Gavin,
   Karen Schirm
Production Director: Douglas M. Johnston
Book Production Managers: Pam Kvitne, Marjorie J. Schenkelberg

Meredith® Books
Editor in Chief: James D. Blume
Design Director: Matt Strelecki
Managing Editor: Gregory H. Kayko
Executive Garden Editor: Cathy Wilkinson Barash

Director, Sales & Marketing, Retail: Michael A. Peterson
Director, Sales & Marketing, Special Markets: Rita McMullen
Director, Sales & Marketing, Home & Garden Center Channel: Ray Wolf
Director, Operations: George A. Susral

Vice President, General Manager: Jamie L. Martin

Better Homes and Gardens® Magazine
Editor in Chief: Jean LemMon
Executive Garden Editor: Mark Kane

Meredith Publishing Group
President, Publishing Group: Christopher M. Little
Vice President, Consumer Marketing & Development: Hal Oringer

Meredith Corporation
Chairman and Chief Executive Officer: William T. Kerr

Chairman of the Executive Committee: E. T. Meredith III

All of us at Better Homes and Gardens® Books are dedicated to providing you with information and ideas to enhance your home and garden. We welcome your comments and suggestions. Write to us at: Better Homes and Gardens® Books, Garden Editorial Department, 1716 Locust St., Des Moines, IA 50309-3023.

If you would like to purchase any of our books, check wherever quality books are sold. Visit our website at bhg.com.

Copyright © 2000 by Meredith Corporation,
Des Moines, Iowa.
All rights reserved.
Printed in the United States of America.
First Edition.
Printing Number and Year: 5 4 3 2 1   04 03 02 01 00
Library of Congress Catalog Card Number: 99-75942
ISBN: 0-696-21030-4

contents

introduction

If you're just starting to garden, *Step-by-Step Garden Basics* is the book for you. And it's so easy to use! Even if you've been gardening a few seasons, you'll find a lot of helpful techniques. ❧We've organized the book by seasons, so whatever the time of year, you can turn to that chapter and see what you should be doing. You'll find everything to get a garden going, whether you want to start seeds

yourself or begin with plants from the nursery, and we tell you

how to get the most out of it all year. At the end of each chapter is a

checklist of garden chores for northern and southern gardeners.

❧With more than 50 step-by-step projects and 100 timesaving

and weather-related tips to guide you, you'll have a beautiful

garden before you know it. There's even space to

record your successes.

Cathy Wilkinson Barash
Executive Garden Editor

Happy Gardening!!

welcome to my garden

cutting gardens

For many gardeners, the greatest luxury is to have an abundance of flowers for indoor arrangements. One way to ensure such bounty is to set up a cutting garden so you don't rob your ornamental garden every time you want to cut some flowers for indoor enjoyment. ❦Although cutting gardens are as diverse as the gardeners who tend them, their main purpose is production rather than landscape display. Often tucked into sunny spaces off the beaten track, cutting gardens are filled with plants that flower exuberantly and dependably. Unlike their ornamental counterparts, these gardens are typically planted in no nonsense rows for easy maintenance and harvest. They may include flowering plants of all kinds—bulbs, perennials, and roses—yet their mainstay is annuals, because they typically bloom for the entire season. The more you cut annuals, the more they bloom. ❦Fill your cutting garden with your favorite plants for bouquets. Include those with a variety of textures and heights and add a few that offer foliage accents. And don't overlook those fragrant blooms.

❦This small patch of flowers is actually a cutting garden. Its jumble of jaunty blossoms with strong stems will continue through most of the summer. You'll stimulate more bloom by taking regular cuttings. You don't have to worry about having a harmonious design and a neat-as-a-pin appearance. Some perennials, such as lilies and coral bells, are so useful in arrangements that they're included with the many annuals. Annual standbys for cutting include nicotiana, phlox, feverfew, cleome, statice, and gomphrena.

ornamental gardens

The best ornamental gardens are a marriage of good design and attractive, appropriate plants. They enhance a residential landscape, setting off the house and other special features of the property. Ornamental gardens may feature perennials, annuals, bulbs, vines, shrubs, or foliage plants—singly or in a pleasant combination. An ornamental garden may take the form of a border or an island bed, and it may be formal or informal, in the sun or in the shade, and parallel or perpendicular to the nearest property line. Choose plants that are adapted to the prevailing conditions in your yard, because these plants will require the least maintenance. And strive for variety—for the many textures and colors and to host a range of beneficial insects and other creatures to control pests and diseases. Year-round ornamental gardens will provide enjoyment in every season if you select plants with different bloom times. Start with spring bulbs and flowering shrubs and end with asters, goldenrod, and trees aglow with fall foliage. Dried grasses and plants with interesting seedpods, cones, bark, and branching patterns continue their show throughout the winter.

9

Not all ornamental gardens feature plants with colorful blossoms. Here the site and soil are best served with foliage plants that share a tolerance for dry soil. The garden's stone edging and the floppy, casual habits of most of the plants create a comfortable, informal style. Wintercreeper, used in the front, provides a bit of color interest with its variegated foliage. As the season progresses, the grasses will change color and develop feathery seedheads. Notice that the taller plants are at the back, the shorter ones in front.

formal gardens

Formal gardens are characterized by symmetrical design and repetition of plants. The simplest gardens are often the most elegant. Typically a formal garden features four similar beds arranged in a geometric pattern around a central focal point. The focal point is usually a statue, fountain, birdbath, or container of plants. Neat, permanent paths of stone, brick, or pavers define the beds as well as direct foot traffic to the center of the garden. The total effect is one of order and neatness. Whether the garden has an herb, a water, or a rose theme, the overall feeling of the formal planting is one of sophistication and tranquillity.

The plants in formal gardens are neatly arrayed within low, tightly clipped hedges that outline each bed. The choice of plants reinforces the restful, elegant tone. Use only a few different plant types and choose subtle (rather than bright) colors. Strive for compact, low-growing shrubs, flowers, or groundcovers and place them around a taller shrub or tree in the center of the bed. For utmost formality, repeat exactly the same layout design in each bed.

Formal gardens need not imitate the rigid style of huge 18th- or 19th-century English or French estate gardens. They may reflect the surrounding environment and have a regional feeling. Here the use of random-sized native stone, laid as a small dry wall to edge the beds, softens the formality while effectively evoking a sense of place. The use of different plants in each bed also contributes to a relaxed country look. Notice how the similar colors of the stone, the house, and many of the plants reinforce the unity of the formal layout.

kitchen gardens

Kitchen gardens are small food gardens conveniently located in a sunny spot usually near the kitchen door. Typically they contain herbs, vegetables, salad greens, and flowers for cutting. Unlike large, classic vegetable gardens, which may be planted far from the house, kitchen gardens are a convenient source of small amounts of fresh-picked food destined for immediate use on the stove or table. Their small scale keeps maintenance at a manageable level. As a bonus, these practical gardens are often ornamental. Whether formal or informal, they can delightfully decorate an entrance—front or back—to the house. Use perennial crops to provide multiseason interest and structure to the garden. The soft, ferny foliage of ripening asparagus stems is a perfect backdrop for the reds and purples of salad greens, basil, and eggplant. A blueberry hedge can shelter the beds while providing flowers and berries, then fall color. Strawberries supply fruit and discourage weeds. How handy it is to duck out the back door to pinch a few sprigs of herbs, such as parsley or oregano. And chives and sage—when allowed to bloom—contribute beauty as well as edible flowers.

This fairly large kitchen garden has a formal layout. Within its brick-edged beds, you'll find globe basil, onions, peppers, many different salad greens, and other crops, all neatly arrayed in rows. The effect is softened by the occasional vertical accent such as the central arch supporting climbing beans and clematis. Containers filled with herbs and flowers punctuate the paths. An attractive fence encloses the garden. You could install a more substantial fence than the one shown here to keep out rabbits, deer, and other critters who like to visit food gardens.

island bed

An island bed stands alone. Unlike flower beds that border walls, hedges, or buildings, an island bed has no back or front. It is often oval, teardrop, free-form, or kidney-shaped. The addition of an island bed can reduce a huge expanse of lawn, unify the plantings on a property, and make good use of limited space and available sunlight. Spacious properties require fairly large beds; otherwise the beds will appear overwhelmed by lawn. Though you may be tempted to carve your island bed out of an open, sunny lawn, you might consider developing it around existing trees or shrubs. It's a simple matter to extend the mulched area under a tree well beyond its canopy and create

The pink flowers in the border complement those in the island bed to unify the landscape. Even though the plants are tall, they don't overwhelm the island, because the lawn between them is wide.

The lower-growing annuals that edge the bed neatly define its gently curving edge. Notice how the lawn path echoes the shape of this side of the bed.

This island bed is planted asymmetrically. Unlike most, it has a definite back and front. Sometimes with an east-west orientation, this is the best way to ensure that the tall plants won't shade the low ones.

a bed that has both shade and sun areas. Incorporate an unobtrusive path, such as stepping-stones, in large beds to give you access to the center. ☙Proportion plays a role in bed size and plant selection. Big beds are suited to large plants, often in mass plantings. Site the tallest plants toward the center of the bed. They should be no taller than half the width of the bed to maintain a balanced design. Working from the center to the edge of the bed, fill in with medium, then smaller plants—small trees, shrubs, perennials, and annuals. In fall, plant hardy bulbs, such as daffodils, tulips, snowdrops, and crocus, for color and interest in early spring. To minimize root disturbance under trees, grow shallow-rooted perennials and groundcovers.

☙Because you can view an island bed from any vantage point, move your yard furniture every once in a while. When you do, you'll have a new perspective to enjoy while relaxing or meditating.

☙A brick walk along this side of the bed supplies easy access and a neat edge. Some island beds have bricks, stones, or pavers of some sort along all sides to define the edges and make lawn mowing easier.

☙In this asymmetrical bed, the taller plants are on one side rather than in the center, creating a less formal look and making it easier to pick the roses.

☙Island gardens reduce lawn size and typical maintenance chores to a more manageable level. Surrounding an island with lawn or greenery sets off the flowers effectively.

13

edible flower garden

An edible flower garden is a double delight: It lets you have your beauty and eat it, too. The trick here is to select only the specific plants whose flowers are documented as safe for humans to eat. Sometimes they're the blossoms of traditional food plants, such as squash, or culinary herbs such as chives. In most cases they're plants that are considered in our culture to be strictly ornamental.

Lilacs, pansies, and tulips are good examples. By growing edible flowers yourself, you can ensure that they're never treated with toxic pesticides. Because more than 70 familiar plants bear edible flowers, you have lots of leeway in creating and planting your own edible flower garden. What's more, it's fun

Nasturtiums are renowned edibles. Their flowers add color and spice to salads, cooked vegetables, oils, and vinegars. Their foliage is tasty, too. Use either dwarf or trailing types.

'Lemon Gem' marigolds are the tastiest of the marigolds, and their foliage has a lemony scent. Sprinkle the flower petals lightly over potato salad or cooked vegetables to create a citrusy, tarragon flavor.

Dianthus, or cottage pinks, are lovely perennials with a sweet clovelike scent and flavor. Chop the petals and mix them into soften sweet butter and spread on bread for attractive tea sandwiches.For a pretty accent, toss petals in with fruit salad.

Thyme is already an herb garden standby. Its foliage is useful in many dishes, and its white, pink, purple, or magenta flowers are good in fish sauces, cheese fillings, and dips.

and easy. Choose a garden style that suits you—formal or informal, island or border, even containers—and dedicate it to ornamental plants that bear edible blooms. It's a good idea to grow several varieties of roses and daylilies, for example, because their flowers vary in flavor. Select and site plants as you would in any garden. Taller ones go toward the back, smaller ones more forward. Don't forget to include vines such as honeysuckle for vertical interest. Use trees and shrubs

that bear edible flowers, such as citrus, roses, and rose of Sharon, to anchor the bed or border. Include herbs, such as sage, borage, mint, and anise hyssop, whose blooms are as tasty as their foliage. Use tiny Johnny-jump-ups, 'Lemon Gem' marigolds, violets, or sweet woodruff for edging.

Chamomile flowers look like miniature daisies, with white petals and yellow centers. Chamomile reseeds easily and can be used as a groundcover, where it will not be stepped on too much, or between stepping-stones of a path. The flowers and foliage smell like green apples. Traditionally chamomile is used to make a calming tea.

Scarlet runner bean flowers easily climb up trellises to provide vertical interest. Use the flowers before they develop into beans. They add a beany flavor to salads and potato and vegetable dishes.

Calendula, or pot marigold, bears yellow or orange flowers. Chop the petals (fresh or dried) and use them as a substitute for pricey saffron; the flavor is slightly bitter. Calendula petals impart a lovely color to cheese, rice, and potato dishes.

15

entry garden

Entry gardens are ever more popular these days, often because new-house designs frequently feature a garage protruding from the front of the home. An area planted around the front entrance to the house softens the impact of the obtrusive driveway and garage and reclaims the landscape from the dominance of the automobile. Regardless of the architecture of the home, an entry garden also establishes the front yard as a welcome transition from the busy world to a tranquil sanctuary. If you decide to add an entry garden, you will find that the same garage that tends to dominate the approach to your house suddenly can become your ally. Its bulk not only

This entry garden is located in California where water resources are limited. The plants—all drought-tolerant and self-reliant—attractively fill an area that otherwise might be a thirsty, high-maintenance lawn.

Attractive lighting fixtures add visual interest to your entry garden—even in the daytime—and highlight the plantings at night. They also augment the light coming from your entry and improve security at the front of your house.

defines a space for a garden, it shelters the area to create a protected niche for plants. Its walls are handy for mounting trellises to support attractive climbing vines or espaliered shrubs. Design your garden to reflect the style of your home. Use similar materials, such as brick or stone, to blend with the surroundings. Choose plants that will be able to handle the soil and light conditions that prevail at the front of the house. If your entry faces south, you know how hot the interior can be in summer, thanks to direct sunlight radiating heat into your walls. You can add beauty outside—and reduce heat gain inside—by planting a small deciduous tree to shade your entry in summer. In winter, after the leaves drop, the sun is a welcome visitor once again.

Use evergreens to anchor an entry garden and provide year-round color. Place taller ones near the back, shorter ones closer to the walkway. Keep the shrubs from crowding the doorway, where they could hide an intruder from view.

Plan to use hardscape materials that harmonize with the plants and the house. Here natural stone forms the walkways. The switch to wood indicates the edge of each step, marking the transition to the next level.

Rosemary, a popular culinary herb that is used here as a groundcover, has soft, needled, green to gray-green foliage year-round in zones 6 and warmer. The plant bears tiny blue or white edible flowers in spring that add color to this bed.

17

country garden

A country garden expresses freedom. In days gone by, wealthy people had a formal city home where they lived during the business week. Plantings there reflected the cramped, disciplined, formal life in the city. These people also had a country place for weekend relaxation and informal entertaining. Their gardens in the country reflected a sense of escape from the confines of city life.

They were informal, and because they were likely to be neglected during the week, they often appeared undisciplined and overgrown. Today country-style gardens are perfect for anyone who loves the relaxed, seemingly carefree abundance of plants and enjoys memories of bygone eras. There are no

This bluestone path contributes to the informal tone of the garden. Stepping-stones, wood chips, or gravel —typically materials at hand— are also common in country gardens. Place landscape fabric beneath them to discourage weeds.

In a country garden, profusion and abundance reign supreme. Here lady's mantle and other low-growing plants spill lazily out of the bed onto the path. They soften its edge, creating the impression that it meanders.

Ornaments or planted containers randomly placed along an expanse of wall or a hedge create variety. Here a pedestal breaks up the stretch of ivy-covered wall. Be sure to include a birdbath in the garden.

special design rules to follow. Country gardens can be any color, size, or shape, and they can be anywhere on your property. However, the best ones have two things in common: color and crowding. Country gardens are all about flowers —as many as possible. Their trademark is a profusion of color, and they're typically jam-packed with exuberant annuals and perennials. Clumps of towering hollyhocks, phlox, larkspur, and cleome with midheight daisies, zinnias, and purple coneflowers are stitched together with luxuriant vines to form an unruly tapestry. Here's an opportunity to experiment with all kinds and colors of plants. And remember, although they may look carefree, healthy country gardens take the same conscientious care that others do.

Tall plants, especially foxglove, are fixtures of country gardens. Their dramatic vertical spires provide a narrow profile and height in the garden that trees usually bring to a landscape. Flowering vines on a trellis or fence post also add height.

Landscape (shrub) roses, rather than more formal hybrid tea roses, casually billow over fences and climb crumbling walls. They provide wonderful color all season long. Cutting the blooms to bring indoors encourages the plants to flower more.

A rustic post-and-rail fence defines the tone and space of this garden. By serving as an extension of an ivy-covered wall and hedge, the fence completes the enclosure. It also provides support for plants growing on either side.

19

border garden

A border garden grows along a boundary of some sort. It follows a fence, retaining wall, deck, building, hedge, walk, or driveway, all of which define the growing bed and provide a backdrop for the plantings. The border softens the edges of the boundary and brightens its appearance. Border gardens are the most familiar and traditional residential garden, probably because they're practical as well as beautiful. Flowering borders solve lots of landscape problems. They effectively obscure the unattractive foundations of a house, deck, porch, or garage. They can beautify the edge of a property and create a sense of privacy. Tall borders—either flowers or

The solid expanse of wall behind this flower border creates a sheltering backdrop for colorful plants. The wall protects them from wind and provides structure for vines. In winter it absorbs and holds heat from the sun.

Colorful annuals, such as this snapdragon, bridge the periods between the peak bloom of perennials when green foliage dominates in the border. If you consistently deadhead the annuals, most of them will bloom steadily all season.

At the front of the garden, use flowering groundcovers such as this sweet alyssum. As they fill in between larger plants, they weave together the elements of the border to provide a more cohesive appearance.

ornamental grasses—screen out unpleasant views and reduce noise and dust from a busy street. Midheight beds can moderate the harsh lines of a swimming pool or parking area. And borders that flow along both sides of a front walkway provide a wonderful welcome. Use all kinds of flowering plants in a border. Mix annuals and perennials (including spring bulbs) to ensure color throughout the growing season. Choose plants that will thrive in the soil and light conditions at the site, remembering that borders work well in both sun and shade—sometimes some of each. Include small flowering shrubs as fillers and trees as anchors for the bed through the entire year. If the border is wide, set stepping-stones or make a narrow path inside the border for access to the back.

Tall, vertical plants normally go toward the back of a flower border. This gladiolus is only a temporary resident near the front. It is grown for cutting and will be harvested soon.

21

Cut down on weeding chores and neaten flower borders by spreading 2 to 3 inches of organic mulch around all plants. It helps retain soil moisture and contributes nutrients as it gradually decomposes.

Border gardens often face a lawn. A small stretch of well-maintained grass beautifully frames the colorful flowers. Maintain a neat, sharp edge between the lawn and garden.

color in the garden

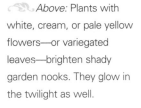

All plants contribute unique ornamental features to a garden. Their leaves, flowers, shapes, and growth habits have their own individual charm and beauty. Many plants produce attractive postseason seedheads, pods, and cones that add even more visual interest. But when it comes to designing an ornamental garden, it's the color—of both flowers and foliage—that matters most. Gardens are more than random assortments of plants you find in nature or orderly rows of merchandise like those you see at the garden center. Instead they're artful arrangements of plants that you purposely select and carefully site to enhance their health and celebrate their beauty. Although you might make your choices for an ornamental garden based on other factors—annual versus perennial, edible versus decorative, woody versus soft-stemmed—flower and foliage color will greatly influence your decision. For some gardeners the goal is simply to assemble a variety of colors in joyous profusion. On the theory that plants of many colors jostle one another everywhere in nature, these

Above: Plants with white, cream, or pale yellow flowers—or variegated leaves—brighten shady garden nooks. They glow in the twilight as well.

Above right: Various patterns of variegation on plant foliage combine with a variety of leaf textures to create an interesting garden that has no flowers at all.

Right: Monochromatic beds—whether developed from flowers or foliage—offer an attractive contrast to a variety of colors. Here shades of green do the trick.

gardeners are comfortable with random color, even though they use other criteria to position the plants. Other gardeners prefer to create a specific effect by using color in a more painterly way. They might, for example, choose hot colors such as red, orange, yellow, chartreuse, and gold for a border garden that receives full afternoon sun. By combining plants with bright-colored foliage and flowers, they create a garden that visually echoes its hot site.

Above: The intensity of colors makes a difference. In this garden the pale flowers—white with yellow highlights—combine with the fine foliage texture to create a lacy, misty effect.

Above right: Plants with bold, highly saturated colors complement one another. When these spring tulips and daffodils fade, the garden may have an entirely different color palette.

bold plants for highlights

Some plants have brightly colored flowers. Others have tall, lush habits. Bold plants have both. Typically they aren't team players, their size and sassy color being too individualistic. They are best used as special effects. They make excellent exclamation points in a border, providing height, vertical interest, or contrast. They're particularly handsome around pools and patios. Many bold plants, such as taro, canna, banana, and ginger, are tropicals. They boast wonderful purple, chartreuse, or striped foliage, and many are topped by flowers in warm, bright oranges, reds, salmons, and yellows. Bring these tender tropicals indoors over the winter in northern regions.

color in the garden (cont'd.)

Conversely these garden "painters" might use cool colors, such as pink, white, magenta, lavender, or purple, for a bed that receives bright but indirect light a lot of the time. In both cases, however, the colors are harmonious. Contrasting colors work just as well. Punctuate a flower bed of warm colors with plants in cool tones. Pair various plants in warm and cool colors, such as chartreuse and purple, in beds or containers. Color plays a key role in special situations such as shade and evening gardens, where plants with pale, luminous flowers or foliage dominate. To attract hummingbirds or butterflies, choose plants with bright, saturated colors.

Above: Nothing says sunshine like a bed of yellow flowers. Single-color gardens (monochromatic) are an interesting novelty. The challenge is to select plants of similar hue and to maintain bloom through the season.

Above right: Nasturtiums are cheery in shades of red, orange, and yellow. Here they make an edible vignette, sparkling as they climb up a cobalt blue trellis and contrasting with lavender flowers.

Right: A harmonious collection of bright, hot-colored flowers brings spirit and liveliness to its part of the garden, whether on the ground or scaling the fence. Gray foliage and the bee skep cool things down a bit.

Below: The blue-based pinkish-purple colors of anise hyssop and cleome set a cool tone for this section of the flower bed. Many herbs, such as sage, lavender, and chives, have flowers in the same color range.

Above: Lilies come in such a wide range of colors that they are naturals for any monochromatic garden scheme. Here pink and white rubrum lilies are paired with hollyhocks and bee balm.

Left: Large properties can handle a tapestry of big, richly colored plants. Here clumps of cool- and warm-colored flowers successfully play off one another to produce a powerful scene that becomes a major player in the landscape.

height in the garden

Flowers growing at graduated heights display the full charm of plants of various sizes. The resulting layers affect proportion and scale in the garden. The flatter the terrain, the more important it is for the garden to have some strikingly upright plants to break the horizon, link the sky with the ground, and relieve the one-dimensional effect of a flat flower bed. The bigger and broader the bed, the taller and bolder the vertical accent plants should be. Their presence forces the eye to move upward and around the garden to take in the dynamic view. In larger landscapes, trees do this. In a garden, tall flowering plants and climbing shrubs and vines accomplish the same purpose. Permanent (hardscape) elements help you create strong vertical lines in your garden. Of course, they add height by

Above: As with most climbing vines, white clematis visually continues the upward reach of flowering plants—in this case the straight, tall foxgloves. The contrasting color and habit of the elements keep the pink foxgloves from blending into the brick wall.

Right: Wisteria can be trained as a self-supporting shrub or as a vine. Notorious as a reluctant bloomer when young, it becomes a real showstopper when it matures. It requires a sturdy support.

themselves, and they make it possible for plants to grow vertically. The wall that defines a border garden, the tepees in a kitchen garden, and the arbor or pergola over a walkway—all enable vines to climb upward. So do statuary and lampposts. Small trees and large shrubs support vines, too. Nothing perks up a ho-hum needled evergreen like a jaunty clematis roaming among its branches all summer. Tall plants, especially vines, soften the edges of a garden. Vines either cling, twine, or grab onto their supports, so choose them carefully. They can hide

landscape eyesores and create attractive transitions between softscape and hardscape elements around decks, garages, and patios. Evergreen vines on the north side of a house insulate it during cold weather. Deciduous vines covering a south wall provide shade, reduce heat gain, and cut glare during the hot summer months.

Left: Rustic, handmade supports are decorative in themselves. Until the peas cover the tepee, it will add height and pleasing proportion to the kitchen garden.

Right: The beauty of roses climbing over an arbor in a flower garden is self-evident. Climbing roses add elegance and height to the scene. Be sure to fasten their canes securely to the support.

27

making a cutting garden

In their prime, cutting gardens are as colorful and lovely as any garden. However, the flowers in this garden are intended to be cut down at the peak of their bloom. Therefore, cutting gardens aren't for display and are usually located off to the side or in the back of the property where they won't detract from the appearance of the yard when the flowers are cut. They exist to provide flowers, foliage, and various seedpods for indoor displays, floral crafts, and gift bouquets. And they provide a generous supply of cut flowers so you don't need to raid the more visible flower border.

Choose a site that receives sun most of the day. Because you'll be placing great demands on the soil,

YOU WILL NEED

- soaker hose
- seeds or seedlings
- gloves
- trowel
- hand pruners
- black plastic
- bucket
- tepid water

1 To ensure regular moisture, lay drip irrigation lines on the planting rows. Soaker-hose (leaky-pipe) systems slowly deliver water directly to roots.

2 Place seeds in furrows, then thin later to correct the spacing. Plant young nursery plants on a cloudy day or at least when the sun isn't bright.

4 In cool regions, warm the soil so annuals can go in earlier. Spread black plastic over the planting rows to absorb the heat from the sun.

5 Start harvesting flowers when plants reach mature size. Be sure to take as much stem as possible and place them in a container of tepid water immediately.

be sure to prepare it thoroughly by adding organic material such as compost before you plant each year. Annuals are heavy feeders because they produce flowers all summer, so dig granular, slow-acting fertilizer into the soil at the beginning of each season. Perennials also benefit from a sprinkling of fertilizer on the soil around the emerging plants in spring to provide consistent, uniform nutrition for several months. Supplement by spraying dilute liquid fertilizer periodically during the summer on the leaves of plants that need a boost Mulch between plants to discourage weeds and retain moisture.

3 Cut off any flowers from young nursery plants. This delays flowering so the plants can channel their energy into building strong roots and stems.

6 Stimulate most annuals and some perennials to produce more flowers by cutting flowering stems as they begin to open. Cut off faded flowers, too.

best cutting-garden flowers

- Baby's breath
- Cleome (spider flower)
- Cockscomb
- Cornflower
- Cosmos
- Dahlia
- Geranium
- Larkspur
- Lily
- Lisianthus
- Marigold
- Mealy-cup sage
- Peony
- Petunia
- Poppy
- Snapdragon
- Sweet pea
- Tulip
- Zinnia

welcome to my garden

planning for paths

Be sure to lay out rows or boxed beds so the paths between them are wide enough to walk on or accommodate a wheelbarrow. As plants grow, they tend to bush out into the paths. Allow enough space so you can lug tools past the plants without harming them. It's important to have easy access to each row for spraying, deadheading, staking, and cutting as well as for replanting with fall bloomers.

29

spring in the garden

starting seeds indoors

Getting a jumpstart on the season is only one of the reasons for starting your own flowers and vegetables from seed. It also lets you try unusual varieties of favorite plants that are available only from seed. In addition seeds are less expensive than commercial seedlings. And having seedlings ready to transplant as soon as the weather permits gives you an instant garden. Finally, if you have seeds, you can plant a fall crop of certain vegetables when no commercial seedlings are available. ❧Chase winter away by getting organized early. To ensure the widest choice, send your seed orders to mail-order suppliers shortly after the new year. ❧Most annuals need six to eight weeks to grow, once they've germinated, before you can plant them outdoors, and some require even more time. Estimate the best time to plant seeds indoors by checking the calendar and counting back from the date you expect the last frost in your area—adding the two weeks it typically takes for seeds to germinate. ❧For the sturdiest seedlings possible, buy commercial seed-starting kits or individual

YOU WILL NEED

- peat pots, cell packs, or flats
- soil-less seed-starting mix, premoistened
- seeds
- indelible marker or pencil
- wooden sticks or plastic plant markers
- plastic cover
- fluorescent lights
- water

1 Fill peat pots, cell packs, or flats with the moistened mix to ¼ inch from their tops. Firm the mix slightly but do not pack it tightly.

2 Sow seeds either by scattering them over the mix or by dropping them individually in rows. Cover lightly with more mix.

seeds to start indoors

plant name	days to germination	time from seeding to planting outdoors
Basil	10	2–3 weeks
Coleus	10	6–8 weeks
Marigold	5	2–3 weeks
Petunia	10	6–8 weeks
Salvia	15	6–8 weeks
Snapdragon	10	6–8 weeks
Sweet alyssum	5	6–8 weeks
Zinnia	5	2–3 weeks

containers made of peat. Water the planted seeds from beneath, to prevent disease. (You can plant peat pots directly into the garden, which minimizes damage to the tender new seedling roots.) A soil-less seed-starting mix is best; it's sterile (which prevents disease) and drains well yet retains necessary moisture. Some of the best seed-starting kits come with plastic covers and a heat mat, which provides bottom warmth that encourages seeds to germinate and grow

well. Seedlings require 12 to 14 hours of daylight —hard to come by in February or March—so you'll need to use fluorescent lights to ensure straight, sturdy stems. Gently brush the seedlings every so often to help encourage healthier growth. Acclimate new seedlings to the outdoors gradually—this is called hardening off—by setting them outside for a few hours, then increasingly longer each day for a week, before planting them in the garden.

moistening the potting mix

Adding moisture to soil-less potting mixes containing peat moss can be a challenge. The trick is to use very warm water. Always add the water to the mix, not vice versa. To moisten an entire bag of mix, put it under a running faucet for a few seconds or pour warm water into it. Let the mix sit for a while to absorb the water. Moisten smaller amounts by pouring the mix into a pan or pail, then adding water and blending it by hand.

33

3 Sow large seeds two or three to a pot. Cover lightly with the mix, unless the seed packet recommends otherwise. When the seeds germinate, snip off all but the single sturdiest sprout in each pot.

4 Use an indelible marker and wooden sticks to label plants in each flat and pot. Include the name of the plant and the date started. Later add the date they germinate and the date planted in the garden.

5 Cover the containers with plastic to hold in humidity until the seeds germinate. Keep the containers out of direct sun and open the cover each day to let in fresh air. Once the sprouts appear, remove the plastic. Position the containers so the plants are about 6 inches from fluorescent lights. Water as needed.

starting seeds outdoors

directly into a prepared garden bed later in spring rather than starting them indoors ahead of time. That's because some plants simply don't transplant well, and others germinate so quickly that there's little to be gained by starting seedlings in advance. And, of course, direct sowing eliminates the need for seed-starting equipment, pots, and the actual transplant process. ❧Oftentimes the hardest part about sowing seeds outdoors is being patient while the soil dries out and warms up. Squeeze a handful of soil to test it. If it sticks together in a ball, it's too wet;

if it crumbles a bit, it's fine for planting. Certain plants, such as pansies, sweet peas, lettuce, spinach, and garden peas, grow best in cool weather. Plant their seeds in early spring, two to three weeks before you expect the last frost. ❧Be sure to wait until there is no danger of frost before planting most other flower and vegetable seeds. They need warm soil to germinate and long days of sunshine to thrive. ❧Direct seeding into the garden is a snap.

YOU WILL NEED

- lime, sand, or sturdy string
- seeds
- pencil or indelible marker
- wooden sticks or plastic plant markers
- water

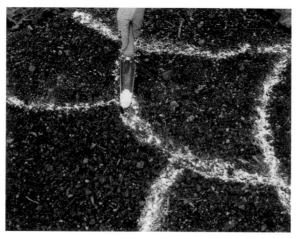

1 After preparing the soil, delineate the planting area with lime, sand, or sturdy string. These markings can be removed later.

2 Scatter seeds on top of the soil or trace straight furrows at the depth specified on the seed packet. Dribble seeds held between thumb and forefinger.

getting seeds to sprout

Some seeds require some help to germinate. Often these are large seeds or those with a thick seed coat. Seeds that need pretreatment include parsley, moonflower, and morning glory. Here are two ways to do this: You can soak the seeds overnight in tepid water. Or you can place the soaked seeds between two sheets of moistened paper or toweling, roll up the paper, and put it in a plastic bag overnight. Check the seeds every morning and evening until they've sprouted *(left)*. Then plant as usual.

However, the new seedlings face natural hazards such as birds, soil pathogens, and rain-compacted or sun-baked soil. A well-prepared seedbed—in which the soil is loose and crumbly and drains well—compensates for some of these difficulties. To duplicate these conditions, loosen the soil, using the appropriate tool (trowel, shovel, power tiller), remove stones, and mix in organic matter such as compost, peat moss, or chopped leaves.

Then add granular, slow-acting fertilizer to provide season-long, consistent nutrition to the plants. Rake the soil smooth. Seeds typically sprout too close together. When they have developed two or three sets of leaves, thin the plants. Remove as many as necessary to establish the spacing recommended on the seed packet. When the plants are several inches tall, mulch the soil between them to discourage weeds.

planting seeds

- *Tiny seeds are more manageable for sowing when mixed with sand.*
- *Large seeds or those with hard seed coats germinate faster if soaked overnight in tepid water prior to planting.*
- *Seeds embedded in tapes facilitate uniform spacing.*
- *Seeds of some so-called hardy annuals, such as calendula, nigella, pansy, poppy, and snapdragon, can be sown in fall, because they can handle winter cold and dampness.*

3 Label areas or rows as a reminder of what's been planted. Sometimes weeds germinate along with the plants you're growing, so labels help to identify the new seedlings.

4 Cover seeds with a thin layer of soil to a depth specified on the seed packet. Firm the soil gently for good contact with the seeds. Some seeds need light to germinate and should not be covered.

5 Moisten the soil if rain is not expected. Use a gentle, fine spray to avoid disturbing the seeds. Make sure the soil doesn't dry out. Keep the young seedlings moist after they sprout, too.

extending the season

Extending the season means lengthening the growing time beyond the regular summer season. If you live in a region with real winters, you'll probably want to stretch the vegetable growing season by starting earlier in spring and ending later in fall. The result: fresh produce from the garden almost year-round. In spring the key is to have the soil warmed and dried out quickly. Most plants and seeds like the soil to be at least 55 degrees F; many need it to be even warmer. You can achieve that by covering the soil with black plastic, which absorbs heat from the sun, several weeks before planting. Protect the transplants by fashioning tunnels of clear plastic over them to admit the sun's

weather

Light frost and hard frost are two different stories. Many plants can survive a brief, light frost overnight and thrive for weeks in the sun of Indian summer. Hard frost is a killer. It freezes the soil and blackens plants. In many regions it signals the arrival of real winter.

For an inexpensive cold frame, set old windows on railroad ties surrounded with bales of straw to keep in the warmth. Prop the windows open for ventilation on sunny days and close them at night.

The curved double-glazed fiberglass top on this cold frame accommodates tall plants. The water-filled black drum at the end absorbs and stores the sun's heat to moderate overnight temperatures.

Commercially made cold frames have hinged tops so they can be opened to allow ventilation when the temperature gets above 40°F.

The cover on the top of this cold frame is made of inexpensive plastic sheeting that's easily rolled up to open the area to fresh air during warm spells.

rays. Be sure to cut ventilation slits in the plastic. Cold frames are useful in extending the traditional season at each end. Set them over planting beds to warm the soil and protect the growing plants inside. Automatic vent openers, available from mail-order suppliers, open the cold frame when it's too warm inside and close it during chilly or cloudy weather. Cold frames also make good transition nurseries for young seedlings awaiting transplanting. A stay of a few days or weeks in the cold frame gradually acclimates them to the outdoors. so they suffer less stress when they're finally planted. There are other

hardening off

Most vegetables are annuals and aren't constitutionally cold-hardy. However, some can adjust to cold if they're gradually acclimated to it, or hardened off. This process happens in two stages. First the cold slows, then stops, the plant growth. Then the plants produce natural sugars in their foliage that depress the freezing point of the water in their cells. This protects them from bursting. Cool-season vegetables have this ability.

This 3×4-foot cold frame is a portable version that's easy to make out of clear plastic sheeting and redwood lumber. It's sized to fit comfortably over a raised bed.

extending the season (cont'd.)

techniques for protecting plants when chilly weather threatens. Cover individual plants with some type of cloche (originally used in France) to trap and warm the air on sunny days. Homemade versions fashioned from plastic milk jugs, old-fashioned bell jars, or terra-cotta pots effectively insulate plants from brief nighttime frosts. Water-filled plastic tepees maintain even temperatures in the soil and around extended-season plants. Throw a light blanket over plants when frost threatens, or use polyspun garden fabric—a lightweight cover that's available in various thicknesses. It allows air, light, and moisture through, but not frost. Mulch effectively

weather

Frost is most likely when the sky is clear and the air is still and dry, with no breeze and low humidity. If the temperature is low already, expect it to drop quickly at sunset. Unsheltered plants may be frosted. Some cool-weather vegetables taste even better after a touch of frost. Kale, collards, arugula, and Brussels sprouts become milder. Root crops such as carrots, parsnips, turnips, leeks, and beets become sweeter after frost.

Plastic milk jugs with their tops cut off fit easily over young plants to protect them from overnight frosts. Weigh them down with stones or bricks in windy weather. Remove the jugs during the day.

Wall O Water™ tepees protect individual plants with water. The water-filled chambers in the plastic support it around the plant. The water collects warmth from the sun and holds it through the night.

Tepee-style cloches accommodate plants as they grow taller. The tops of the tepees are vented to prevent overheating. As the plants increase in height, they can poke out the top.

Recycle panes of glass as shelters for plants. When fastened together with aluminum clips, they form a tent to trap heat from the sun. The space at the top of the glass provides ventilation.

insulates the soil and protects plant roots. Spread a 2- to 3-inch layer of organic material such as chopped leaves, straw, aged wood chips, or pine needles on the bare soil. ❧Try to maintain soil warmth as long as possible to extend the gardening season into fall. Plastic covers (for beds and rows) or a cold frame allows you to grow a second crop of cool-weather vegetables such as chard, broccoli, and spinach. There's nothing like fresh vegetables from the garden for Thanksgiving dinner.

❧Loosely throw polyspun garden fabric over beds of early-spring or late-fall crops if a light frost threatens. Temporarily weight the edges with bricks or stones. Remove the cover the next morning.

❧Row tunnels made of plastic protect entire rows of warm-season vegetables from late-spring frost. The black plastic floor warms the soil, and the clear plastic top collects and holds warm air.

building a plastic tunnel

To use a plastic tunnel, the plants you want to protect must be in raised growing beds that are boxed in. Collect your building materials: 1-inch flexible PVC pipe, string, and a roll of plastic. Bend the PVC pipe into hoops or ribs and insert them into the soil every 3 to 4 feet. Link them with a length of string tied at their tops and along both sides to stabilize them. When weather conditions require action, cover the unit with plastic or polyspun garden fabric (also known as garden fleece or floating row cover) and anchor it firmly to the ground. Tunnels covered with clear polyethylene plastic help extend the growing season at each end. In spring they protect newly planted tomatoes and other warm-season crops while they become acclimated to the outdoors. If frost is still possible, stretch a sheet of the plastic or polyspun garden fabric over the hoops. Use stakes, soil, or a row of bricks or rocks to anchor it at the sides and ends. Be sure to cut ventilation holes in the tunnel. When frost arrives for sure in fall, keep the cover on crops that are still producing.

transplanting seedlings

After a period of gradually acclimating to the wind and sun outdoors, young plants are ready to go into the garden. This process can be traumatic for the plants, so try to choose an overcast day or wait until late in the day to plant. This spares the seedlings extra stress from bright sun while they cope with the inevitable transplant shock. Their adjustment is much easier, too, if their new soil is loosened, moist, and reasonably warm. Dig a hole for each seedling about the size of its pot. Tip each plant from its container, tapping the bottom to dislodge it if necessary. If its roots are encircling the root ball—because of confinement in the pot too long—loosen them by hand or cut vertical slits in the root ball. Set each plant in a hole at the same depth that it grew in its pot. Then gently but firmly press the loose soil around the plant to seat it in the ground and force out any air pockets, then sprinkle with tepid water. After a week, water the new transplants with water-soluble plant food mixed at half the strength recommended on the label.

spacing plants

One way to avoid problems as seedlings mature into full-sized plants is to allow sufficient space between them when planting. Although the garden may seem bare at first, giving plants the room to grow without being crowded ensures good air circulation, which deters diseases. Mulch the bare soil between small plants to discourage weeds from filling the space while the seedlings grow.

Set small plants in rows to edge beds. Screen an undesirable view with a row of tall plants. Plant flowers in rows for convenient cutting.

Ornamental plants make an impact when grouped. Odd-numbered clusters work best—three large plants or up to nine small ones per group.

aftercare

- Water newly transplanted flowers and vegetables every day or two in warm weather until their roots grow deeper in the soil. When they show new stem and foliage growth, you'll know that their roots are established properly.

- Spread a 2-inch layer of organic material on the bare soil between the young plants. This mulch will discourage weeds and help keep the soil moist.

- Pull any weeds that appear in the planting area. They compete for water and soil nutrients.

- Early in the season watch for unexpected temperature drops. Have polyspun garden fabric handy to cover the transplants if frost threatens.

- Insert stakes into the soil or erect trellises for plants that will need support.

- Inspect plant foliage regularly for insects or disease. Pinch off tender plant tips, if necessary, to eliminate clusters of aphids.

- As transplants mature, pinch off stem tips to increase side branching and compactness.

Tuck young transplants into existing beds
among flowers that require the same amount of
light and water. Do not crowd them.

choosing nursery-grown plants

- Purchase plants at a reputable nursery or garden center, where they're likely to receive the best care.

- Buy early when the plants are fresh and young.

- Check for moist soil and perky foliage to determine that the plants have been properly cared for.

- Choose plants that are compact and stocky, with firm stems. This means they've received good light.

- Look for leaves that are a rich green and free from discolored spots or signs of insects.

- Examine the plant's roots by slipping it from its pot. The roots should be well developed throughout the potting mix but not tightly tangled or trailing out of the bottom hole of the pot.

- Select plants that are in bud but not fully flowering. Younger plants transplant more successfully than older ones.

- Check to be sure that all the plants in a market pack or flat are healthy.

planting vegetables

Production is the name of the game in growing vegetables. The current trend is toward smaller yards—and, therefore, less space to grow food crops—so planting patterns greatly influence the size of the harvest. A wide-row layout is the most efficient way to take advantage of available growing space, because it uses areas formerly devoted to paths between narrow rows of plants. This wider planting area becomes, essentially, a bed. Make a bed any length, but limit its width to 3 to 4 feet across so you can reach the center of the bed from either side. Although it's not necessary to box in the bed, this is a good idea anyway. When you enclose a bed with vertical boards, it's not only neater, but the

YOU WILL NEED

- string
- small sticks or dowels
- trowel or dibble
- seedlings
- water

1 Before planting, run lines of string to establish a grid. The grid will help you position young plants at the proper distance from one another.

2 Use a trowel or dibble to dig holes. Gently remove the seedling from its container. Grasp the leaves to guide it while supporting the root ball.

3 Set the plant in the hole at the same depth at which it was growing in its container. Firm the soil gently over the roots around the stem. Water well.

4 As this layout demonstrates, any given plot will accommodate many more plants when arranged in a grid pattern rather than in narrow rows.

soil won't collapse onto the paths. Also, it will be much easier for you to install row covers or erect supports for vertical growing. Prepared soil that's protected in beds is superior, because it's never compacted by foot traffic. ❧Before planting the bed, prepare the soil by digging down at least 12 inches (18 is even better) and turning over shovelfuls to loosen and aerate it. Mix in organic matter, such as compost or manure, and granular, slow-acting fertilizer. Remove stones and debris, then rake the area smooth. This creates a raised mound of loose, rich, crumbly soil for wide-row planting.

rotating crops

Crop rotation helps control disease and insect problems. Plant crops in different places each year to thwart pathogens and pests that overwinter near their host plants in the soil. For instance, plant this year's tomatoes in a different bed from last year and put green beans where the tomatoes were. In small gardens, even moving plants just a few feet away from last year's location helps.

43

5 Save space in the garden by helping crops to grow upright. Various structures can support peas, pole beans, melons, cucumbers, and tomatoes.

planting vegetables (cont'd.)

Good soil is the key to good production, regardless of what you're growing in your backyard vegetable garden. A rich soil supports intensive plantings of various crops and sustains successive plantings. If soil is rich in organic matter and is never compacted by foot traffic, plant roots grow deeply and vigorously. In the superior soil of a raised bed, it's possible to plant more intensively than normally recommended. Set plants closer together so that at maturity their leaves will just touch those of neighboring plants. This helps shade the soil as well. Although each head of broccoli may not be as large, there will be more of them. You can further

weather

Although the last spring frost is usually around the same time every year, there are always surprises. Cool-weather crops such as broccoli and lettuce can handle a frosty morning. Protect young warm-season plants with clear-plastic tunnels, cloches, or polyspun garden fabric.

Lengths of black plastic sheeting laid over prepared planting beds in early spring will warm up the soil. Most warm-season vegetables require soil to be at least 55°F.

Cut slits in the plastic to dig individual planting holes and allow water to reach the soil. Set each plant in a hole, then firm the soil around its stem by pressing gently on the surrounding plastic.

Either direct-sow seeds or transplant seedlings into rows in a prepared garden bed. Temporarily mark straight rows with sprinkled lime or string fastened to stakes.

When the plants are a few inches tall, thin them to the correct spacing as indicated on their seed packet. They need good air circulation and enough space to grow well.

increase the yield if you interplant a variety of crops. Plant beets with broccoli. Beets grow rapidly in spring while broccoli is getting established, and they are ready to harvest about the time the maturing broccoli plants shade the soil and need more space.

Intensive planting uses every cubic inch efficiently—both on the surface and in the air. Choose climbing varieties, such as pole rather than bush beans. Vertically grown plants thrive because they're exposed to abundant sunshine and good air circulation.

Randomly broadcasting seeds of some crops, such as lettuce mixes or mesclun, over a section of prepared bed works well. Try it with carrots or spinach. Thin sprouts regularly as they mature.

Different crops require different spacing. Intensive planting in raised beds allows closer growing than specified on the seed packet. Thin young plants or plant seedlings with that in mind.

mulch for low maintenance

Mulching the soil is an important gardening technique.

- Mulch helps control soil temperature. When summer heat raises the soil temperature too high, plant growth stalls. A layer of organic material will cool the soil several degrees.

- Mulch also discourages weeds, which compete with seedlings for soil moisture and nutrients. By covering the soil, mulch prevents weed seeds from germinating and protects the soil from compaction by rain and hot sun.

- Mulch helps retain moisture by blocking evaporation from the soil surface. The spongy humus in organic mulch also absorbs rain, reducing waste through runoff. At the same time, it prevents splashing of soil-borne disease pathogens from the soil surface onto plant leaves.

- Decomposing organic mulch helps keep the soil alive. As the mulch breaks down, it contributes humus, which is teaming with microscopic life. These organisms—along with earthworms—process soil nutrients.

45

succession planting

Plant crops in prompt succession by using wide-row planting in beds to produce more food. Dig up the plants as soon as their main production is over and replace them with seedlings for a different crop. As the weather warms, cool-season crops such as peas are completing their production. Have young squash or cucumber plants ready to take their place on the trellis. As soon as the broccoli is finished, have tomato plants ready to take its place in the bed. A planting area that's never idle produces a surprising amount of food. ❧Another type of succession planting is repeating the same crop over a period of time to stagger the harvest. You can avoid being inundated by an entire crop all at once by planting only a few beans, then waiting two to three weeks before planting more, then more even later. Unless you intend to freeze the crop, your harvest will be more manageable if you spread it over many weeks. Plant lettuce, carrots, and other favorites this way, too. ❧Soil that produces a steady flow of produce over several months needs help, because a succession of

YOU WILL NEED

- sharp scissors
- trowel
- young transplants
- slow-acting fertilizer
- water

thinning

❧After seedlings have developed two or three sets of leaves, they'll be crowded and need thinning. Remove extra plants to achieve the correct spacing and allow the remaining plants room to grow.

❧Thin a crop of young plants by snipping off the stems at the soil surface. For larger plants, this is preferable to pulling them, when you might damage the roots of neighboring plants.

spacing plants

plant name	spacing between plants/seeds	thin young plants to...
Beets	1 inch	5 inches
Carrots	1/4 inch	2–3 inches
Corn	3–4 inches	6–10 inches
Lettuce	1/2 inch	10–12 inches
Peas	1 inch	don't thin
Peppers	12–18 inches	don't thin
Summer squash	in hills	3–4 feet
Tomatoes	18–24 inches	don't thin

your own gourmet vegetables at home

The baby vegetables that are popular in restaurants are easy to have fresh from your garden. You can harvest many vegetables (with the exception of tomatoes and eggplants, for example) when they're small.

- When planting the garden, look for varieties that tend to stay small.
- To spur production, pick often. At season's peak, this may mean daily trips to the garden.
- Harvest peas, beans, and cucumbers regularly to keep them coming.

crops inevitably depletes the soil of nutrients. They must be replaced to maintain production over the entire season—plus an extended season. Mix a granular, slow-acting fertilizer into the soil when you first prepare the bed. This food provides a large portion of the nutrients needed for plant growth over several weeks. Depending on the product, it may last for 12 or even 16 weeks. Its continuous action releases essential nutrients consistently and uniformly. Plants get a steady, balanced diet. You may want to add fertilizer again midway through the season. Vegetable plants may be annuals, such as peppers or potatoes, or perennials, such as rhubarb or asparagus. Because perennial vegetable plants stay put year after year, they aren't involved in succession planting. They can't benefit from rotation, either, so be sure to fertilize and mulch their beds to ensure continued good health.

foliar feeding

Plants that produce heavily over a long period, such as tomatoes, benefit from a snack to augment their main meal of slow-acting fertilizer. Periodically over the season, spray a dilute liquid fertilizer or kelp product on their leaves to give the plants an energy boost.

47

continuous planting

Immediately replace exhausted early-season crops with seedlings for the next crop. This follow-up procedure, called succession planting, achieves maximum production from the garden space.

Between succession plantings, cultivate the soil to aerate and level it. Clean up old plant debris before replanting. Add granular fertilizer if previous crops, such as tomatoes, were heavy feeders.

cool-season crops

Cool-season vegetables can handle the chill of early spring and late fall. They fade rapidly when the warmth arrives in early summer and eventually succumb to freezing in winter. They're ideal for extended-season growing. Vegetables that don't mind being chilly, such as peas, broccoli, and spinach, make it possible for you to have two crops a year—one in spring, another in fall. Often the second crop, at the onset of winter, is the one that you're happy to put into the freezer.

try these cool-season vegetables

- Broccoli
- Brussels sprouts
- Cabbage
- Cauliflower
- Collards
- Garlic
- Kale
- Leeks
- Lettuce
- Onions
- Peas
- Spinach
- Swiss chard

planting flowers

Flowering plants may bloom annually or perennially. *Annuals* are genetically programmed to live their entire life cycle in one season. They sprout from seed in spring, then mature, flower, set new seed, and die (when frost arrives). Although some may tolerate light frost, they're unable to withstand temperatures below freezing. Annuals are remarkable for their flower production—virtually nonstop over the season. Many leave behind their seeds to grow and bloom the next season. *Perennials* are more permanent plants. They live for many years, their roots developing gradually to support increasing top growth over several seasons. The majority are able to withstand winter weather in most regions, although some are "tender" perennials and do not survive in far-northern winter climates. Perennials bloom for only

planting bare-root perennials

YOU WILL NEED

- bare-root plants
- shovel or trowel
- water

1 Unpack mail-order plants immediately and check them carefully. Look for damaged roots and, if leaves are present, signs of insects or disease.

2 Plant bare-root perennials promptly. Dig a hole in prepared soil and form a hill or cone of packed soil at the bottom to support the roots.

3 Spread the roots on the cone and cover them with soil so the crown—where the roots join the stems—is level with surrounding soil. Water well.

a limited time each year. The remainder of the season their foliage collects energy from the sun to build strong roots for next year. Annuals and perennials are sold by mail order and at garden centers. Young plants may be in flats or cell packs that hold four to twelve or more. Older plants are typically in individual pots. Plant them as soon as possible after you buy them. Be sure to keep the soil moist if there's a delay. Trim off any broken stems or damaged leaves. If the plants come in plastic pots, knock them out of the pots before you put them in the ground. Take pains to keep the soil and roots intact as the plants go into their holes. Plant those that come in peat or coconut-fiber pots directly into

benefits of flowers

Adding flowers to a landscape improves the health of all plants. A variety of bright and colorful blossoms attracts many beneficial insects, most of which especially like open, daisylike blooms. These predatory insects, which are virtually invisible, attack and kill other insects that not only threaten plants but carry diseases that can cause even more damage.

49

special handling for taprooted perennials

Some bare-root perennials, such as this Siberian aster, have a long taproot. Plant them deeply.

Plants may have either taproots or fibrous roots. Both depend on the root hairs to take up water and nutrients from the soil and pass them to the main root system. Carrots are a good example of a taprooted plant. So are dandelions, butterfly weed, and balloon flower. In taprooted plants, root functions are concentrated in one main root. This tapered, thick structure grows and elongates as it penetrates deep into the soil. Because the root hairs are concentrated on this structure, don't break off a part of it, because you may doom the plant. This makes taprooted plants a challenge to transplant. Consequently they're typically sold as young transplants. It's too chancy to dig and package them for sale when they're mature and the taproot is large, because the root is so brittle that it's easily damaged when handled.

Move a spade back and forth to make the hole. Then position the taproot and press the hole closed.

Handle young plants with taproots very gently. Carefully choose a place for these plants, because they won't tolerate being moved once they are established and grow larger. All taprooted seedlings are fragile. If they've been field-grown, their roots may have been damaged when they were dug up. Plants that are raised and sold in peat pots, which can go directly into the ground, pot and all, are best; the plant is least disturbed by the planting process. Keep transplants moist until planting time. Place taprooted plants in soil that has been deeply cultivated. This enables the root to grow downward freely. Soil that's compacted, has heavy clay, or contains large stones impedes root growth and causes stress. Before planting, add organic matter, such as peat moss or compost, to improve soil texture.

planting flowers (cont'd.)

the prepared bed. Follow the same procedure outlined on pages 40 and 41 for transplanting seedlings. Perennials sold by mail order usually arrive dormant—still in their winter rest cycle and without any leaves. Some are shipped bare-root rather than in pots with soil. Their roots are wrapped in moist sphagnum moss, wood shavings, or similar material. The absence of soil eliminates the chance that soil-borne diseases will be passed across state lines. These plants also weigh less, reducing the cost of shipping. It's likely that they were grown outdoors in real soil, so their roots are well-prepared for transplanting into your own soil.

planting container-grown plants

YOU WILL NEED

- container-grown plants
- garden shovel
- trowel
- knife
- water
- organic mulch

1 Prior to planting, set container-grown plants on the bed to determine the best placement. Odd-numbered groupings look most natural. Allow space for perennials to mature and spread each year.

2 Dig a hole large enough to accommodate the root ball when it's removed from the container. Set the plant in the hole so that the top of the root ball is level with the surrounding soil.

3 Gently tip the plant out of the pot. If necessary, tap the bottom of the pot with a trowel handle to free the plant. Loosen tangled roots and make vertical cuts in any that are circling the root ball.

4 Set the plant in the hole and fill in around the roots with soil. Firm the soil, then water well. Mulch the bare soil around the plant with chopped leaves, compost, or other organic material.

Site the transplants—both annuals and perennials—where the available light suits their needs. Water them as you plant them, then continue watering on a regular basis, particularly if rainfall is limited in your area. Sufficient moisture will help them cope with the stress of having been shipped. Don't fertilize them until you see their ready signal: new leaf or stem growth. Some plants will grow tall and need support. Set stakes near them in the soil while the plants are young to avoid root damage.

easy-to-grow perennials

The plants listed below are widely available at retail outlets across the country. They're also recognized within the perennial plant industry as well as by gardeners across America as reliable and sturdy.

- **'Sprite' Astilbe –** a diminutive hybrid astilbe with glossy dark green foliage. It produces sprays of shell pink flowers in midsummer shade gardens.

- **'Moonbeam' Coreopsis –** small, eight-petaled pale yellow flowers grace the tips of thin stems covered with narrow leaves. It blooms all summer in full sun.

- **'Palace Purple' Heuchera –** boasts handsome deep purple foliage all summer in partial shade. It bears tiny, pale bluish-white flowers clustered at the ends of wiry stems in spring.

- **Creeping Phlox –** neat, deep green foliage on creeping stems mats to cover the ground in woodland settings. In spring it produces clusters of small florets in white, blue, or pink.

- **'Sunny Border Blue' Veronica –** offers a strong, vertical accent for the garden and bears spikes of rich violet-blue flowers in summer. It does best in a sunny site.

- **'Magnus' Purple Coneflower –** jaunty, daisylike flowers with droopy purple petals bloom in midsummer when many other perennials are idle. It thrives in full sun.

- **'Goldsturm' Black-eyed Susan –** provides billows of late-summer daisylike golden blossoms with dark centers on coarse, hairy stems.

diagnosing plant symptoms

Plants give clear signs when they aren't healthy. Inspect them for symptoms at the nursery before you purchase them. Examine their foliage, stems, and roots. Choose only those plants that appear to be sturdy and vigorous. Beware of bargain plants that may have been neglected or kept too long on the shelves at the garden center.

- **Yellow or wilted leaves –** neglect; lack of water, light, or fertilizer

- **Spotted or discolored leaves –** possible fungal disease

- **Lower leaves fallen onto soil in pot –** irregular watering; temperature stress

- **Dark marks or blotches on the stem –** injury or disease

- **Specks on undersides of leaves –** possible insect infestation

- **Spindly stem –** insufficient light

- **Lots of flowers, few buds –** overfertilization and/or advanced age of plant

- **Weeds in the container –** nutrients not getting to plant due to weed competition; infertile soil

- **Roots emerging from container –** plant outgrowing its pot

dividing perennials &

If you divide your perennials and bulbs, you'll keep them looking their best. By *not* doing so, you force them to spread into large clumps and crowd their space. As a result, flowers are smaller, leaves lack good access to light and air, and roots become tangled and massed. Then their overall health declines, because individual plants are less able to absorb nutrition from the soil. This makes them weaker and vulnerable to pests and disease. ❧You can protect them from crowding: Every few years, cut large clumps into smaller pieces for replanting. This also gives you an opportunity to examine the roots and bulbs for rot or insect damage. Often the center of the plant mass grows woody; if this is the case, you can discard it after you cut away the younger, more vital parts of the plant. ❧Division is

dividing and replanting daylilies

YOU WILL NEED

- shovel, spade, or trowel
- sharp knife
- water

weather

Don't depend on fickle spring rainfall to water replanted divisions adequately. Like any transplant, they need regular moisture while their roots struggle to establish at a new site. Water them well at planting time and every day or two thereafter.

1 Divide daylilies by digging and lifting a clump with its root ball. Cut back leaves for easier handling. Shake off excess soil to expose the roots.

2 Use a sharp knife to cut down through the roots and separate a chunk of plant. Be sure it has at least one "fan" of leaves, complete with good roots.

3 Set daylily divisions in the ground at the same depth at which they grew before. Spread the roots in the hole, fill the hole with soil, then water well.

bulbs

the best way to maintain plant health and optimum size for the garden, as well as increase the number of plants. It reliably produces plants that are exact replicas of the parent, and at no cost. A single large hosta or clump of daylilies will yield several small chunks of rooted plants. Place them elsewhere on the property or give them away. ◥A bed of iris or daffodils can become crowded, because the mother bulb develops offshoots, or bulblets. Gently separate the bulblets from the mother bulbs, then replant the mother bulbs at the correct spacing. Now you can move the bulblets to new sites. You may have to wait another year or two for them to mature and produce flowers.

daylily care

The newer reblooming types of daylilies need frequent division. These hybrids are programmed to produce a great flush of blooming stems in spring. Then they send up several new stems and continue to bloom throughout the summer. For the best performance from 'Stella d'Oro', 'Happy Returns', and others, divide them every two to three years. To increase their blooms even more, pinch off dead flowers promptly.

dividing and replanting iris

1 Dig each crowded clump of iris rhizomes, then trim the leaves back to 5 inches. Separate healthy plants with good roots from woody, damaged ones.

2 Set the healthy rhizomes in a shallow trench, roots downward. Cover the roots and half of the rhizome with soil so the other half shows above the soil.

3 Plant small rhizomes about 3 to 4 inches apart in beds. Position them so that their fans of leaves are oriented in the same direction.

dividing perennials & bulbs (cont'd.)

Divide most perennials as soon as they begin to show growth above the soil. Because their roots have been dormant all winter and are just starting to grow, they won't experience much shock during the process. Wait to divide spring bulbs until after they bloom and their leaves ripen and die back. Dig and divide plants that need rejuvenation after they bloom. (Read about dividing perennials in fall on pages 100–103.) Pay close attention to the type of roots the divided plant has and how deep they grow. Make sure that each division from the main plant has sufficient roots to support it. Gently tease divisions apart from the mass, ensuring

dividing in place

Another way to divide plants is to do it in place. Sometimes the clumps have gotten too large to dig comfortably out of the ground in order to gain access to the root ball. Ornamental grasses are a good example. Dig down with a sharp spade into the planted clump, cut pie-shaped chunks out of the root ball, and remove them. The main plant is undisturbed. Fill in the hole with soil, and water well.

dividing and replanting daffodils

1 Dig up crowded clumps of daffodils in spring. They are one of the few bulbs you can divide while their leaves are green. Gently tease the tangled roots apart to separate the bulbs.

2 Lay the bulbs on the soil as you want to plant them in the ground. Plant them in natural-looking drifts rather than in soldierly rows. Space bulbs 4 to 6 inches apart.

3 To plant lots of bulbs, use a long trowel especially designed for bulb planting. Insert the trowel 4 to 6 inches deep and rock it forward. Drop the bulb in the hole, pull out the trowel, and tamp down the soil.

that each one has at least two buds from which the new growth will sprout. Replant them at exactly the same depth at which they were growing before. Peony buds should be just visible at the soil surface. Plant them any deeper, the peonies won't bloom.

volunteer seedlings

1 On some plants, such as hellebores, flowers left to fade and set seed will self-sow. To prevent this, you can pinch or cut off spent flowers promptly. Or look at it as a way to get lots of new free plants.

2 Carefully dig up the seedlings and tease apart the roots. Replant them in another suitable area of the garden, or plant them in individual pots and give away to friends or share with other gardeners.

perennials to divide in spring

Always divide plants after they flower. For spring-blooming perennials and bulbs, this usually means early summer to early fall. For summer- and fall-blooming perennials, this usually means spring. After the plants die back in fall, their roots rest in dormancy over the winter. Then in spring the plants begin to send up new shoots. When they have only a few inches of growth, they're easy to handle. The replanted divisions are young and resilient and have plenty of time to recover and become established before it's time to bloom again.

good candidates

- Aster
- Astilbe
- Bee balm
- Black-eyed Susan
- Chrysanthemum
- Coreopsis
- Daylily
- Goldenrod
- Hosta
- Liatris
- Ornamental grass
- Phlox
- Purple coneflower
- Sedum 'Autumn Joy'
- Veronica
- Yarrow

55

planting trees & shrubs

Trees and shrubs are significant investments that can repay you with years of beauty and enjoyment. If your house needs relief from summertime sun, a row of tall shade trees can do just that. One of the major keys to success in growing healthy trees is choosing the right sites. Survey your yard for locations that will offer plenty of sun and adequate space to grow. If you follow a few planting techniques carefully, you should have healthy, beautiful trees. Whether they come from the nursery with bare roots, wrapped in burlap, or grown in containers, keep them moist until you can dig them into the ground. The best planting times are spring and fall. It's vitally important to plant

planting a balled and burlapped tree or shrub

YOU WILL NEED

- shovel
- balled and burlapped plant
- water
- chopped leaves or compost
- tree wrap (optional)

aftercare

To ensure that a tree or shrub survives transplanting, water it well for at least three months. In cold-winter climates, keep watering the plant until the ground freezes.

1 Dig a saucer-shaped hole with sloping sides about twice as wide as the burlap-wrapped root ball. Dig as deep as the root ball is high. Do not put loose soil into the hole.

2 Set the wrapped root ball in the hole. Loosen the burlap so that the root flare at the base of the trunk is visible. It must be level with or slightly above the surrounding ground.

4 Use soil to form a dam around the planting area. Water in and allow it to drain. Spread a 3-inch layer of chopped leaves or compost over the root zone.

5 Temporarily protect the tender bark from sunscald or animal damage by wrapping vulnerable limbs with tree wrap.

trees at the correct depth. If they're deeper in the soil in their new location than they were where they grew before, they'll suffer stress, which invites disease and pests. ❧Experts no longer recommend routine staking of new trees. Their trunks need to flex to grow strong.

3 Position the tree to your liking and make sure the trunk is vertical. Cut away as much of the burlap as possible—it may be synthetic and resist decay. Fill the hole with ordinary soil and firm it. Add water.

❧There are different types of tree wrap—paper, plastic, and woven material. Wind the wrap in overlapping layers like a bandage.

planting a containerized tree or shrub

1 Dig a wide, saucer-shaped hole with sloping sides as deep as the plant container. Do not amend the soil from the hole unless the ground is hard clay. Delay fertilizer for six months.

2 Tip the plant from its container. Loosen or clip off extremely tangled roots. Check for proper depth by setting the plant in the hole carefully without disturbing the root ball.

3 The plant should be at exactly the depth that it was in its container— just level with or slightly above the surrounding ground. Partially fill the hole with plain soil, then add water.

4 Add more soil; firm over the root ball to eliminate possible air pockets. Water again. Spread a thin mulch of chopped leaves to discourage weeds and hold soil moisture.

5 Small shrubs and trees may need protection from browsing deer and gnawing rodents. A cage of hardware cloth will deter critters while the plant becomes well established.

YOU WILL NEED

- shovel
- containerized tree or shrub
- water
- chopped leaves or compost
- hardware-cloth cage (optional)

57

planting bare-root roses

Hundreds of varieties of roses are featured at local nurseries or in mail-order catalogs. These days, many roses—especially landscape (shrub), rambling, and old garden roses—come planted in containers, already in bloom. Plant them following the suggestions for planting containerized shrubs (page 57), allowing 4 to 6 feet between plants. Hybrid tea roses and their cousins—floribunda and grandiflora—typically are shipped bare-root and dormant. Their canes have no leaves—but buds are visible where leaves will soon appear—and their roots are wrapped in moist paper or sawdust. Because the roots easily dry out, be sure to keep them wrapped and moist until you're ready to

YOU WILL NEED

- bare-root rose
- pail
- water
- compost or other organic material
- gypsum (optional)
- shovel
- heavy gloves
- pruners
- mulch

1 Soak bare roots in a pail of water overnight. Prepare the soil in the planting area by adding compost or other organic material. Ensure good drainage in heavy clay by adding gypsum.

2 Dig the planting hole about 2 feet deep and wide enough to fit the roots and several inches of stem. Fill the hole with water to test for drainage. It should drain within an hour.

5 Set the roots on the soil cone so the swollen graft union is 2 inches below ground level (but at ground level in areas with frost-free winters).

6 Partially fill the hole with soil. Water, then fill the hole to ground level. Mound soil around the crown temporarily to keep the canes moist.

plant. ❧Site roses carefully. Once established, they resent being moved. Grow hybrid teas and their cousins in a bed of their own. Their stiff canes and upright habit don't blend well with other plants. They need frequent attention and rich soil, which is easier to provide at one location. ❧All roses need protection from wind and at least six hours of bright sun daily. Sunlight dries their leaves, reducing the chance of fungal disease. In hot climates, some shade from afternoon heat is welcome. Space hybrid teas at least 24 inches apart so you can prune and cut the flowers without fighting the thorny canes.

quality roses

Since 1938, All-America Rose Selections (AARS) has encouraged rose growers to improve the vitality, strength, and beauty of roses for America's gardens. At trial plots around the country, promising new varieties are observed for superior vigor, bloom, and disease resistance under controlled conditions. Those selected as AARS winners have the AARS emblem on their package labels and stem tags. Look for this sign of quality.

3 Prune any roots broken during shipping or packaging. (Be sure to wear heavy gloves.) Even after you've done this, each plant still should have three or four healthy canes 8 to 10 inches long.

4 Use loose soil to form a tall cone at the bottom of the hole. This will support the bare roots in the correct position—and in proper alignment in the hole—until the hole is backfilled.

7 Create a water reservoir over the roots by firming a ridge of soil around the perimeter of the planting area. Fill it with water to soak the soil.

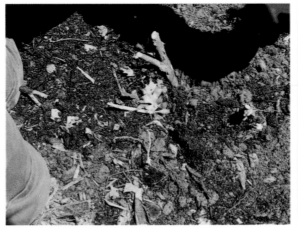

8 Spread mulch over the planting area. Prune canes by one-third to stimulate new growth. Make cuts just above a swollen leaf bud that faces outward.

planting strawberries

Growing strawberries is easy and rewarding.
Their bounty sweetens the arrival of summer. You can buy several types, each with a different production schedule. Mix and match these varieties for a season-long harvest. ❧ June-bearing plants are the traditional ones. They produce abundant fruit in early summer in one major harvest period, then stop producing. Everbearing types, in spite of their name, bear two separate crops each year. The first is in June, the second in fall. The latter is a heavier crop, but the berries are typically smaller. Because everbearers require a fairly long growing season, they aren't recommended for northern regions where winter comes early. ❧ Day-neutral strawberries produce all summer. They aren't dependent on the short days and cool weather that conventional strawberry

YOU WILL NEED

- shovel or trowel
- dormant crowns
- water

protecting the harvest

When strawberries start to ripen, songbirds quickly go after the juiciest red fruits. Cover the beds where berries are ripening with plastic mesh, netting, or polyspun garden fabric. For better access at picking time, drape netting over flexible PVC pipes that have been bent as ribs over the bed. Anchor the edges of the fabric with bricks or stones.

1 Form a cone of packed soil at the bottom of each 6-inch-deep hole. Set each strawberry crown on a cone and flare its roots down the sides.

2 Make sure the crowns—where the roots meet the stems—remain above the soil level after each hole is filled and the soil is firmed.

5 Strawberry plants bear flowers and set fruit simultaneously. Peak harvest time in northern climates is usually June. Some types bear all season.

plants require. ❧Certain strawberry varieties get along better in some regions than others. Garden professionals or your local Cooperative Extension Service can guide you. Otherwise all types of strawberry plants have relatively similar growing requirements. ❧You can buy them from garden centers and mail-order suppliers in late winter.

They're typically sold as dormant crowns—bundles of dried, pale roots. Plant them as soon as the soil is workable. (If they arrive before you can plant them, store them in the refrigerator.) Strawberries like a well-drained, weed-free planting bed. Add organic matter, such as compost, manure, or peat moss, to prepare the soil and improve its drainage.

aftercare for June bearers

Attend to June-bearing plants every year to maintain strong health and production. Mow or clip off their leaves after harvest to forestall fungal disease and stimulate new growth. (Adjust the lawn mower so that it doesn't cut their crowns.) Cultivate the soil between rows, then spread granular fertilizer and water it in. In several weeks, expect plants to send out lots of new runners, which will root and establish new plants.

3 Space plants every 12 inches in rows 18 inches apart. Pinch off runners the first year. Thereafter allow them to root for a solid mat of growth.

4 Strawberries flower and set fruit the first season. To increase eventual production and build plant vigor, pinch off the flowers the first year.

alpine strawberries

Unlike their cultivated cousins, alpine strawberries do not send out runners. Instead they form compact mounds that are perfect for edging around vegetable, herb, or flower beds. They, too, need a sunny site and well-drained soil. Alpine strawberries are easily grown from seed. Their fruits are small (only ½ to 1 inch long), sweet, and intensely flavored—similar to wild strawberries. This luscious fruit is available with red or pale cream berries and is also ornamental when planted in hanging baskets and traditional terra-cotta strawberry jars. Alpines continuously bear their treats from midsummer on and will produce for many years.

supporting vegetables

and training vegetables to grow upright, away from the soil surface. They take up less space in the bed, making room for you to intensively plant other crops. The taller plants are healthier, too, because their stems and leaves get better air circulation, which reduces the chances of fungal disease. Moisture from rain or overhead watering dries off more quickly. Their fruits receive more sunshine so they ripen sooner and more evenly, and they're cleaner and more shapely. Certainly they are less likely to contract rot diseases or injury by soil-dwelling insects. And, finally, they're easier to harvest. Some vegetables are born to climb. Peas

weather

The winds and heavy rain that accompany summer storms are a threat to plants. Make trellises and other supports sturdy enough to withstand these conditions. Supports holding plants laden with fruit at the peak of the season are especially vulnerable because they carry so much weight.

Vining crops such as peas and pole beans grow nicely on wire-covered A-frame structures. When the produce is ready for harvest, it will be within comfortable reach from either side.

Support individual tomatoes or other tall plants by driving 8-foot stakes at least 12 inches into the ground. Plant a young transplant near each stake and loosely fasten its stem with soft strips of fabric.

Firmly insert wire cages into the soil to give tomatoes good support as well as access to air and light. Wide openings make it easy to pick the fruits.

Not all support structures need to be tall, such as this cucumber netting. Check seed packets and plant labels for information on the mature height.

and cucumbers have tendrils that take to a trellis with gusto. Tomatoes have flexible stems that can be tied to or woven through wide mesh. Pole beans naturally wind around stakes or any other vertical structure. In the case of melons and squashes, a double support works best. Encourage the vines to climb a sturdy trellis, then cradle each large dangling fruit—as it reaches maturity—in an individual sling. Do this by cupping a length of polyspun garden fabric, netting, or even old panty hose under the melon or squash, then fastening each end to the trellis netting.

tomato types

There are two types of tomato plants. ***Determinate*** *types grow only about 4 feet tall and stop. They don't need a tall trellis. A sturdy wire cage suits them fine. They also do well in containers with attached supports.* ***Indeterminate*** *types will grow as high as 20 feet if you let them. Make a 6- to 8-foot support for them— whatever is within maximum reach—and clip off the tips of the main stems when they reach that height. This promotes subsidiary branching and more production.*

63

trellis placement

Orient trellis panels on a north-south axis so that tall vines don't shade other shorter plants.

🌱 Wooden lattice panels, their base deeply embedded in the soil for solid footing, provide an attractive support. Small pea tendrils cannot wrap around it, so place netting in front of the trellis.

🌱 Wire or nylon mesh with 4-inch openings allows for easy picking of peas, which in this garden are followed by tomatoes.

🌱 Build a freestanding tepee sturdy enough to hold several vines. Anchor it firmly in the ground to stand up to strong winds. It should be 8 to 10 feet tall.

supporting flowers

Flowering plants are ornamental and add wonderful color and texture to your landscape. Although some yards are informal—with flowers spilling willy-nilly out of beds and over fences—many plants in this setting look best if they are supported. Such plants will benefit from more sunlight and better air circulation, and their flowers are less likely to be splashed with mud or their stems broken in rainstorms. Take advantage of the enormous number of commercial staking devices, or make your own. Choose a support appropriate to each plant's habit and shape. Train climbing stems while they're tender and flexible. To prevent root damage, insert stakes near plants when

keeping vines in line

Some vines, such as moonflower, can grow up to a foot a day, so make sure it's growing where you want it. Check often for stems or tendrils that wander off-limits.

twining vines

Some vines twine around a support in either a clockwise or counterclockwise direction. If you're training such a vine (morning glory, pole bean, or moonflower, for example) and it falls off the support after you've wrapped it in one direction, wind it the other way.

Support branching plants, such as these purple coneflowers, by inserting sturdy stakes around the perimeter of the clump. Zigzag string from one stake to another to form a support matrix for the stems.

Metal ring supports, commonly used with peonies, also discipline clusters of supple stems that tend to flop. Use the supports temporarily around clumps of daffodils and freesias.

Reinforce tall plants in beds with individual stakes or a string matrix attached to stakes located around the entire perimeter of the bed.

Sometimes a row or two of string fastened to stakes around the outside of a plant clump, such as these black-eyed Susans, does the job.

they are young. Set matrix or ring-type supports for clumping plants early in the season, so the burgeoning stems can grow through easily. Inspect and repair permanent devices before plants begin their climb. Above all, make sure all supports are extremely sturdy.

Secure tall plants such as lilies or delphiniums to stakes with loose twist ties or soft yarn in figure-eight loops. Avoid root damage by inserting stakes into the soil near each stem when the plant is young.

You can purchase single-stem metal supports with easy-open loops to hold an individual flower stem, such as a lily, loosely and inconspicuously.

supporting vines

Fasten simple wooden "rungs" to a wall as a permanent ladder-type support for this mandevilla and other vines. Weave the stems along the support before they become woody.

Some vines will grab onto any object without encouragement. For an informal look, let sweet peas, clematis, and morning glory wrap their tendrils or stems around whatever is handy.

A few vines will obligingly climb horizontally, too. Train a clematis, such as this, to attach to rails or picket fences. Because roses cannot cling, fasten their canes with twist ties.

Arbors and pergolas are meant to be vine-covered. Guide young stems toward the base of the structure. Annuals, such as morning glory and lablab, bloom most of the summer.

Vines thickly established on a trellis create privacy and screen out unwanted views. Perennial vines will provide a mantle of leaves after their bloom period is over.

summer in the garden

container gardening

Growing flowers in containers offers endless possibilities. No matter how restricted your space, you can always find room for interesting containers stuffed with colorful flowers. They work everywhere. In the garden they provide focal points and accents. Container plantings make attractive transitions between the yard and the pool or patio, literally bringing the garden close to the house. They beautify vacant areas on a deck, draw attention to special landscape features, and decorate doorways, steps, walls, and niches around the house. Plant a morning glory in a container and set it on a wall or railing to drape all summer. Cluster interesting pots of various sizes and plantings for an instant

planting annuals in a strawberry jar

YOU WILL NEED

- soil-less potting mix, premoistened
- slow-acting fertilizer
- water-saving crystals (optional)
- strawberry jar
- trowel
- young plants
- pruners
- water

1 Mix moistened potting mix, fertilizer, and optional water-saving crystals together. Add the mix to a strawberry jar up to the level of the lowest pocket.

2 Snip off flowers to ease stress from transplanting. The plant roots will develop faster in their new home if they do not have to support flowers, too.

3 Tuck a plant into each pocket, starting at the bottom. Add potting mix through the top of the jar to cover the roots of each plant as you work your way upward.

4 Top off the pot with a slightly larger plant. Water enough to settle the mix around the roots of all the plants. Add more mix at the top, if necessary, after the water soaks in.

garden. ❧Part of the fun of container growing is deciding which plants to combine to get maximum effect. Experiment with lots of combinations by replanting pots several times to coordinate with season changes. Pull out spent spring bulbs and tired pansies when summer arrives and add a riot of petunias, geraniums, cannas, and begonias. Change plants again for fall by introducing chrysanthemums, marigolds, celosia, and coleus. Because all but the largest containers are portable, you actually have a mobile garden that can redecorate a new spot in minutes. ❧Containers full of flowers can solve

containers

Almost anything that holds soil and drains water will work as a container for plants. Traditional-style pots are available in a variety of materials, among them plastic, resin, stone, concrete, wood, glass, wire, metal, ceramic, and, of course, terra-cotta.

In addition you can have fun by making your own pots out of recycled and found objects. As you visit gardens, you'll be amazed at the range of containers that people use—from old boots (with the requisite hole in the sole for drainage) to battered rowboats (perfect for a seaside garden even if you live inland). Recycled tires turned inside out and painted elaborately are a far cry from the old tire on the lawn.

Disguise plain plastic pots by putting them inside decorative jardinieres or antique containers. Add a few inches of pebbles under the plastic pot if the ornamental container does not have a drainage hole. Check it after a heavy rain to see if it needs emptying.

plants for hanging baskets

Try these handsome trailing annuals for hanging baskets:

- *Black-eyed Susan vine*
- *Browallia*
- *Flowering oregano*
- *Ivy geranium*
- *Kenilworth ivy*
- *Lantana*
- *Madagascar periwinkle*
- *Mexican cigar plant*
- *Nasturtium*
- *Portulaca*
- *Petunia*
- *Vinca*

71

container gardening (cont'd.)

problems, too, by disguising drainpipes, covering bare spots, and screening utility boxes. They brighten up quiet corners and add beauty to areas under trees and roof eaves where you may find it difficult to plant in the ground. ꕷAll kinds of nursery items grow well in containers—from trees and shrubs to vegetables, herbs, and bulbs. Annuals are most satisfactory because their shallow, fibrous roots adapt easily to a crowded pot. They're available with a variety of brightly colored, long-blooming flowers or striking silver or variegated foliage. Because annuals are relatively inexpensive, it's easy to replace them when they fade. ꕷSet

planting a hanging basket

YOU WILL NEED

- basket liner
- water
- wire-form hanging basket
- scissors
- potting mix, premoistened
- slow-acting fertilizer
- water-saving crystals (optional)
- trowel
- young plants

water-saving crystals

Sometimes even a good potting mix is no match for hot summer days. You can add water-saving polymer crystals to the mix before planting. They absorb water and slowly release it as the soil dries.

1 Wire-form hanging baskets must be lined with an appropriate material—in this case, coconut fiber. Soak the liner overnight to soften and moisten it. Cut slits in the liner so it fits snugly.

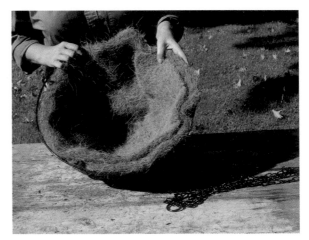

2 Line the frame with the circle of coconut fiber, then press it into the wire form. Take care not to squeeze too much of the water out of the liner. Trim off or fold over any liner that extends above the rim.

4 Make sure that all of the plants you've chosen share the same light requirements. If the basket will hang in a shady spot, you'll want to choose shade-loving flowers and ferns.

5 Use a trowel to insert plants into the potting mix, starting in the center and working your way outward. Place the plants closer together than recommended for a garden bed.

container plants near the house— nearby, they're more convenient to check daily, especially in summer, to be sure they have enough water. Plants in terra-cotta pots or hanging baskets dry out especially quickly. If there is no slow-acting fertilizer in the potting mix, add dilute, water-soluble fertilizer to the watering can every other week. Pinch back leggy stems to encourage compactness as the season progresses. Keep polyspun garden fabric handy to cover the container in case a light frost is forecast.

3 Fill the lined basket with premoistened potting mix. Add slow-acting fertilizer and/or water-saving polymer crystals to the mix to cut down on watering and feeding later.

planting a tub

You can plant a wooden tub with a profusion of color in no time at all. Although it's not necessary to line the tub with plastic, you'll extend the life of the tub by doing so. A black plastic trash bag works well. Be sure to punch drainage holes in the bottom before placing it in the empty tub. Roll or cut down the sides of the bag so they're below the lip of the tub. Fill the bag with premoistened potting mix. If the mix doesn't already contain some slow-acting fertilizer, add some to it now to give plants consistent, uniform nutrition over many weeks. Because a round container is often viewed from all sides, plan your design with that in mind. Start planting at the center and working toward the rim. Set the tallest plant in the middle to create a vertical line. Then set medium-height plants around it. Really cram them in. Make a final ring of small plants around the edge of the tub, and tuck among them some vining types that will droop or trail over the side.

6 Because hanging baskets are often viewed from below, add hanging or trailing types of vinca, petunia, nasturtium, or geranium at the rim of the basket. That way, beauty comes from all directions.

identifying garden pests

A typical landscape teems with insects, fungi, bacteria, and other organisms, most of which are benign or beneficial if the environment is healthy. Only a small number of insects and organisms are harmful. The trick is to know good from bad. Most of the time, populations of harmful insects and pathogens are kept in balance with the good guys. However, sometimes this balance is tipped because of weather, pollution, or the death of beneficials from overuse of pesticides. The usual result: a population explosion of undesirables. Infestations might show up as blemished or chewed leaves, clusters of bugs on buds or tender stem tips, and/or rotted roots. Some diseases, such

pesticide alert

Broad-spectrum chemical pesticides often cause more

problems than they solve, as seen on this damaged plant. Because the pesticides kill indiscriminately, they destroy beneficial insects, too. Then when pest insect populations rebound, there are no predators in the garden for several weeks to control them.

fungal diseases

Blackspot is a fungal disease commonly found on the foliage of hybrid tea roses. Spores splashing up from the soil during a heavy rain create moist, infected dark spots that are easily visible.

Powdery mildew, a gray coating of fungus on leaf surfaces, appears when plants are crowded and lack good air circulation. Humid summer weather encourages mildew.

Holes can indicate a number of different problems. Before using chemicals indiscriminately, identify the pest that has caused the holes.

Botrytis is a fungus that creates water-soaked spots on food crops and ornamental plants. The spots, once enlarged, become covered with grayish mold.

as bacterial and viral infections, kill plants quickly; the problem and outcome are never in doubt. But fungal diseases, such as mildew and blackspot, rarely kill a mature plant. Sometimes ants signal trouble by congregating around the sweet liquid produced by pest insects feeding on infested plants. Yet you shouldn't assume that because you see ants congregating around a plant that there are problems. For example, ants are always found on peonies just before the flowers open. In that case the ants are actually eating a substance off the bud that helps the flower open. Good bug or bad?

beware of bugs

Rose caterpillars, the larvae of a number of moths and butterflies, chew holes in or skeletonize rose leaves and flowers. Leaf-roller types curl the leaf edges around them.

Japanese beetles (green and copper wings) chew holes in plant foliage. Their soil-dwelling larvae—plump, curled, cream-colored worms with brown heads—eat grass roots.

Colorado potato beetle larvae are humped blackish worms that chew foliage. Adults (yellow with black stripes and orange heads) lay bright yellow eggs on leaf undersides.

Aphids are soft-bodied, pear-shaped, and tiny with long antennae. Colors may be green, black, brown, or pinkish. They cluster on new plant growth and suck juices from the cells.

Snails and slugs may be brown, black, yellow, or gray. They lurk in dark, moist places during the day and sustain themselves by chewing on plant fruit and foliage at night.

Leaf miner adults are minute black flies. Their yellowish larvae tunnel between leaf surfaces, marring them with pale tracings. These insects sometimes carry disease.

controlling garden pests

The first defense against insect-related problems is to keep plants healthy and happy. A stress-free plant has its own effective defenses against attack by insects, caterpillars, and beetles. Sometimes, though, plants are unable to fight back. The best way to limit damage and preserve plant health is to catch the infestation early. Several times a week, walk through the garden and routinely inspect your plants. Check young ones and tender new growth on others—both likely victims for insects that suck plant juices and chew on leaves. Try to catch and treat plant pest problems early to prevent the diseases that often strike plants weakened by insects. Some insects even carry disease that they

insecticide alert

Use all insecticides— even those labeled "organic" or "natural"— with respect. Follow the instructions on their labels for use, storage, and disposal. Always protect skin and eyes; when using powdered products, wear a pollen mask.

fungicide recipe

An effective spray for blackspot and mildew is a mixture of 1 teaspoon of baking soda, 2 drops of vegetable oil, and 2 drops of dishwashing liquid in 1 gallon of water. Spray the top and bottom of the leaves at the first sign of a problem. Don't spray if the temperature is going to be over 80°F.

Japanese beetle traps, with their pheromone and floral lures, attract beetles from a wide area. Hang bags at distant corners of the property.

Insecticidal soap kills soft-bodied insects on contact by penetrating and dissolving their tissues. Spray it on aphids, whiteflies, and mealybugs.

Floating row covers temporarily protect plants from insects. The polyspun garden fabric allows light, air, and moisture to penetrate but bars insects. Remove it to allow pollination of food and flower crops.

Water spray is effective against aphids, mites, and mealybugs. It can disrupt their life cycle when directed at the spots where pests congregate—stems and both sides of the foliage.

introduce into the plant as they feed. Make sure that the insects are actually pests and not beneficials, such as parasitic wasps, ladybug larvae, and soldier beetles. When in doubt, leave them alone. Beneficial insects (which you can buy at garden centers or mail order) can often handle the problem. However, if infestation should threaten to overwhelm a plant or garden bed, you'll need to intervene. Start with the least toxic measures such as traps, handpicking, or a forceful spray of water. Then turn to light horticultural oil, neem, or insecticidal soap sprays. Remember that they kill the good bugs as well as the bad.

reducing plant stress

Plants that are happy seldom suffer from pest or disease attacks. Stress from environmental conditions, such as too much sun, too much or not enough water, and wind or storm damage, tends to weaken a plant's natural resistance. Competition from weeds, excess fertilization, and compacted soil also stress plants. Protect them from stress as much as possible. Mulch and water them during times of drought, and prune damaged stems or faded flowers.

Slug traps can be as simple as a slate or board laid on the ground. During the day, slugs seek shelter from the sun. Scrape them off daily.

Wire cages are effective against pest animals such as squirrels, birds, rabbits, woodchucks, and deer. More utilitarian than decorative, they're most often used in the vegetable garden.

good bugs

Spiders help control pest insect populations by preying on their eggs in the soil. A thick lawn cut at 2½ to 3 inches tall shelters and protects them.

Lacewings feed on pollen and nectar produced by plants. Their larvae are predators of aphids, mites, scale, mealybugs, whiteflies, and other offenders.

controlling weeds

Weed seeds lurk in almost all soil. Most weeds don't cause a problem because they never get the light they need to germinate. However, when you cultivate ground for planting, weed seeds inevitably surface and sprout beside the new plants. From the outset, weeds compromise the health and welfare of ornamental and food crops by crowding plants and competing for nutrients and moisture. They often harbor disease pathogens as well as insects and their eggs. The best way to prevent weeds is to cover the soil with mulch to deny the seeds of annual weeds and the emerging perennial weeds the light they need to grow.

To be effective in thwarting weeds, a material used

weeding tips

- Remove weeds as soon as they appear, while their roots are undeveloped.
- Use a regular hoe or scuffle hoe to scrape the surface of the soil to dislodge the tender sprouts—roots and all.
- Take care not to disturb the roots of nearby shrubs and plants.
- Rake up the weed seedlings or leave them lying on top of the soil to dry out in the sun.
- Never put any aggressive weeds on the compost pile.

mulches

Straw is an ideal mulch for vegetable gardens, where appearance is not critically important. It easily allows moisture through, cushions ripened vegetables that drop, and doesn't decompose for many months.

Small stones allow moisture and air through to the soil. They also hold heat from the sun to moderate nighttime soil temperatures. However, they don't improve the soil.

Cocoa hulls make a handsome, fine-textured cover. They allow air and moisture through to plant roots. And they smell like chocolate!

Pot shards block sun from weeds and retain moisture. Their color attractively sets off certain ornamentals. But shards don't feed the soil.

as mulch must block light yet allow air and moisture into the soil to benefit the roots of nearby garden plants. There are all sorts of mulches, such as landscape fabric, decorative gravel, and colored plastic, but the best mulches are organic—plant material that eventually decomposes. Organic mulches are superior because they improve the soil as they discourage weeds. Over time they break down into a spongy humus teeming with living organisms, which enrich and condition the soil. Plants mulched with straw, chopped leaves, grass clippings, or other organic matter benefit from this bonus.

handpicking weeds

Handpick larger weeds (including those you missed on other weed patrols) that are growing in or around ornamental or food plants. Wait until the soil is moist. Grasp the weed stem at the soil level between your thumb and forefinger. Pull with a steady, gentle pressure to coax the entire root out of the ground. Mulch the area immediately to prevent the emergence of more weeds.

Shredded bark gives a neat, finished look to soil around landscape plantings. It holds up well for months before gradually decomposing to enrich the soil. Replace it each spring.

Compost offers the ultimate in soil enrichment and blocks light from weed seeds in the soil. However, seeds that blow in from elsewhere readily take root in this mulch.

Shredded leaves make an excellent mulch and are a good way to recycle leaves from your yard. They effectively block weeds and enrich the soil.

Pine needles have a finished look and lovely color. They control weeds effectively, break down slowly, and are ideal for plants that like acidic soil.

harvesting vegetables

Most food crops reach their peak flavor and nutritional value when they're still young and tender. As they approach maturity, these qualities begin to deteriorate. The seeds inside fruits and vegetables develop and ripen, causing the skins to become thicker—and their stems tougher—to protect the seeds inside. The optimum harvest time is just before that happens. Because different vegetables mature at different rates, the trick is to be ready to pick each crop at its prime. This might mean picking asparagus and tomatoes daily, and eggplant and lettuce every five days or so. You'll want to harvest ripening peas and pole beans every couple of days to ensure continuous

harvesting bell peppers

Harvest time makes a big difference with bell peppers. When they mature to full size, they are green but still have a bitter flavor because they're not fully ripe. Allow them to remain on the plant and ripen further for several more weeks. When they become red, yellow, or orange, they're sweeter. Because the peppers take so long to change color, individual plants don't produce as many peppers over the season. You may want to increase the number of plants to maintain production levels.

Turnips planted in midsummer provide a delicious harvest throughout the fall. Their flavor improves with a chill. Dig them up with a spading fork when they're 2 to 3 inches in diameter.

Asparagus is a perennial and sends young shoots up early each spring. Cut them at soil level with a sharp knife before their tips begin to mature —looking like ferns as they branch and leaf out.

Cauliflower is ready to cut from its stem when the head is firm and tight. It will deteriorate within a week or two of reaching maturity.

Zucchini are ready for harvest when they are 5 to 8 inches long. You'll find them at their peak flavor and tenderness at this young age.

production over the season. ⛛The time of day when you pick the garden's bounty is important. For most fruits and vegetables, early morning is best, because that's the time they have maximum starch (for sweetness) and crispness from the cooler, overnight temperatures. Pick them right after the dew dries.

Eat or store freshly picked produce promptly. If you allow vegetables to sit on a counter for hours, they lose moisture and vitamin content. To prevent their continued ripening, put them in a plastic bag in a cool, dark cellar or refrigerator. Never wash them before storing, because the moisture encourages rot.

avoiding fungal contamination

As a general rule, avoid picking crops when plants are wet from dew or recent rain. This is when fungal diseases, various mildews, and rots flourish and are most likely to spread. Avoid brushing against infected fruit or foliage, then moving from plant to plant while picking, because this will transmit fungal spores onto healthy plants. Dampness makes them vulnerable to infection.

🌱**Fingerling (or new) potatoes** are ready for digging when the plants finish blooming. Dig the potatoes, spread them on the soil to dry, then brush off the soil and store them in an airy, cool, dark place.

harvesting tomatoes

The ultimate harvest moment is when the first tomato of the season is ripe. Depending on the variety and when the plants were put into the garden or an outdoor container, this might be in early July. Although determinate tomato varieties are genetically programmed to grow and produce for only a certain period of time, indeterminate ones continue producing fruits until frost. Tomato stems are tough, so harvest the tomatoes with garden scissors or pruners rather than just yanking them off the vine. For best flavor, pick ripe tomatoes just before you're going to eat them. If you're picking a few days' worth of tomatoes, store them out of direct light at room temperature. Green (unripe) tomatoes will ripen on the kitchen counter.

encouraging blooms

Most people think of pruning shrubs and trees when this subject comes up. However, the judicious cutting away of part of a plant is just as important to the health and performance of annual and perennial flowering plants as it is to their woody cousins. Techniques called *deadheading* and *cutting back* are really just types of pruning, and both are invaluable in maintaining flowering plants in a garden setting. They're also the best ways to encourage plants to deliver the most and best flowers for the longest possible time. There are lots of ways that pruning can encourage plants to bloom. If you cut back entire stems when they become leggy, you will stimulate the plants to replace them with new, vigorous growth that will eventually produce more flowers. Because you're eliminating worn and possibly damaged parts of the plant, you're also doing away with potential sites for disease or insect attack. This ensures that the plant will live out its natural life span and produce a maximum number of

attracting birds

Leave some flowers to dry into seeds for the birds to eat in fall and winter. They especially like black-eyed Susan, purple coneflower, bee balm, amaranth, thistle, and other plants with large seed heads. Of course, sunflowers are the all-time favorites, keeping birds fed well into the snowy months.

Disbudding—or removing certain buds as they form on plants such as peonies—directs energy to the remaining ones, producing larger flowers.

Delay cutting back faded blooms and bare stems of plants and you'll be rewarded with interesting seedpods. The seeds of money plant are perfect for dried arrangements.

self-sowing flowers

You usually can count on these flowers to reproduce themselves:

Anise hyssop	Four-o'clock	Nicotiana
Blanket flower	Foxglove	Nigella
Calendula	Garlic chives	Scilla
California poppy	Hollyhock	Sweet alyssum
Chamomile	Johnny-jump-up	Tall verbena
Cleome	Marigold	Tiger lily
Columbine	Morning glory	

flowers. You can extend the life span of some biennial plants well beyond the normal two years by cutting their flower stems immediately after they bloom. Use sharp pruners and cut the stems cleanly to promote healing. ◀Cutting stems partway is less drastic than removing them completely. Moreover it forces plants to send out side branches. Cut back just far enough to remove a cluster of faded flowers and bare stem down to the next leaves. New growth will obscure

the cut, make the plant bushier, and provide more lateral stems to flower. The flowers may be smaller, but they will be more numerous. ◀Deadheading—pinching off individual blooms that are dead or dying—extends the bloom period by promoting repeat blooms. Because plants are intended to set seed, removing the flowers before they can accomplish that causes the plant to produce more flowers and try again to complete its life cycle.

pruning tools

Sharp pruners and garden shears make clean cuts. This is important because clean cuts heal faster, making plants less vulnerable to disease. They undergo minimum stress and look neater. Choose pruners with bypass blades rather than anvil-type blades, which tend to crush stems as they cut.

Deadheading flowers—promptly pinching or cutting off those flowers that have faded—stimulates a plant to produce replacement buds and more blooms. It improves the plant's appearance, too.

Deadheading flowers and stems—a practice that makes sense when you encounter long, bare stems—is appropriate for this black-eyed Susan. Cut back to where leaves emerge from the stem.

Cutting back means cutting major stems back to the foliage at soil level. This removes all the spent flowers and old stems, stimulating the plant to send up new stems with fresh buds.

encouraging blooms (cont'd.)

Annuals typically respond to deadheading enthusiastically, by diverting the energy that they would have devoted to making seeds into making new flowers. Deadheading also prompts certain perennials to complete the development of buds lower on the stem that might otherwise never bloom. To remove faded flowers on tender stems, simply pinch their stems between your thumb and forefinger and pull sharply. Sometimes it helps to press with your fingernail. If the stem is too tough, as with many perennials, use scissors or pruners. You can apply the same pruning techniques to foliage plants as well. Pinching off flowers, cutting back to the next leaves or trimming to the ground stimulates the plant to produce new stems and fresh, young leaves. In the

disbudding

You can manipulate a plant's bloom size or bloom pattern by using a process called disbudding, which involves the selective removal of flower buds from a plant. For example, if you remove the terminal bud, you will induce the plant to produce more—but smaller—flowers than normal on side shoots. If you remove side buds, you'll encourage the plant to create a larger single terminal flower.

Deadhead plants to eliminate unwanted blooms. Pinch off flower heads from coleus to encourage desirable foliage and stall the plant's aging process.

Encourage branching by pinching off flower heads. The plant responds by producing new stems off the main stalk, giving it a bushier look.

Deadhead drifts of low-growing groundcovers, such as sweet alyssum, by shearing spent blossoms all at once. This revitalizes the entire planting.

Stimulate new flowering within weeks in a patch of damaged plants by cutting back affected plants to healthy stems with foliage.

case of coleus, where the flowers detract from the effect of the varied and colorful foliage, deadheading maintains leaf production. In plants where foliage is edible, such as basil, lettuce, or parsley, pinching and cutting back to eliminate flowers prevents the foliage from becoming bitter. Although these actions benefit plants, they also cause temporary stress. Plants must rally to heal wounds and start to develop replacements for the lost foliage and flowers. Give them a light dose of fertilizer and plenty of moisture to help them rebuild tissues and maintain continued or increased bloom for the remainder of the season.

no deadheading needed

Some annuals deadhead themselves. They're sometimes described as self-cleaning plants. Their faded blossoms, often small to begin with, shrivel, dry, and drop off of their own accord. The next rain washes off any that have temporarily stuck to the foliage on their way to the soil. These plants, including wax begonia, impatiens, cleome, morning glory, and nicotiana, quickly generate lots of replacement flowers.

Some roses put on a spectacular show in June, then spend the rest of the season soaking up sunshine to prepare for next year. Prune off their spent blooms to improve their appearance and prevent disease. Other types, such as low-maintenance landscape and rugosa roses, keep flowering even with spent blooms on the plant. Hybrid tea, grandiflora, and floribunda rose varieties require regular deadheading for best summer-long production. Clip off spent flowers to a junction of five or more leaflets along the stem.

a cutting garden

A cutting garden is more practical than it is ornamental. Its gorgeous, colorful flowers certainly look beautiful, but they're there only temporarily. This type of garden is grown to be cut down. It's a production facility, where flowers are a crop you'll be using for indoor arrangements, gifts, floral crafts, and sometimes even cooking. Often tucked behind the house or inside a fence of its own, a cutting garden never has to be in display condition. In fact it's typically planted in space-saving rows or beds designed for regular harvesting. ❧Lots of different kinds of flowering plants are suitable for a cutting garden. For fresh-cut bouquets, choose those that have sturdy stems and a long vase life such as lilies, zinnias, and snapdragons. For dried-flower crafts and arrangements, plant flowers that easily air-dry and hold their color. As you plan your layout, be sure to site the plants so that the taller ones do not shade the smaller ones. And try to place similar flowers in groups, for easier harvest. After you cut them all, clear up the area and put in a new crop.

flowers for cutting

These flowers are traditional favorites for cutting gardens:

- *Aster*
- *Baby's breath*
- *Blue salvia*
- *Celosia*
- *Chrysanthemum*
- *Cleome*
- *Cosmos*
- *Daffodil*
- *Dahlia*
- *Delphinium*
- *Goldenrod*
- *Larkspur*
- *Lily*
- *Nicotiana*
- *Snapdragon*
- *Statice*
- *Sunflower*
- *Tulip*
- *Zinnia*

❧Long-stemmed flowers, whether perennial or annual, are the most popular and useful for cutting gardens. All types of daisies are big favorites and combine well with lots of other flowers. Silver-leafed artemisia and herbs, such as lavender and sage, have silver foliage that is both handsome and aromatic.

❧Include all kinds of flowers in a cutting garden—early-season bulbs, spring annuals, summer bulbs and flowers, and fall-flowering plants. To ensure a steady supply of gladiolus, plant bulbs every few weeks. Don't forget plants with interesting foliage, pods, and seed heads.

Plant annuals in succession for maximum yield. As soon as you cut one stand of blossoms, pull the plants, cultivate the bed, and add seedlings for the next cutting. Or devote one bed to mature plants, a second to those on the brink of maturity, and a third to young plants—ensuring a steady supply over the entire growing season.

regional summer checklist

	Perennials	**Trees and Shrubs**

Cool Climates

Perennials

- [ ] Deadhead faded flowers to groom plants and stimulate rebloom later in the season. Allow self-sowers to retain their last blooms.
- [ ] Spread a 2- to 3-inch layer of organic mulch, such as chopped leaves or pine needles, over bare soil between plants to discourage weeds, keep the soil moist, and enrich the soil as it gradually decomposes.
- [ ] Promptly pull any plants that show viral or bacterial disease. Remove the nearby soil as well. Then disinfect tools with a mixture of hot water and household bleach.
- [ ] Routinely inspect plants for pest problems. Knock Japanese beetles off foliage into a jar of soapy water. Keep the hose handy to spray off aphids and mites.

Trees and Shrubs

- [ ] Prune spring-blooming shrubs and trees, such as azalea, rhododendron, magnolia, and forsythia, as soon as blooming is over to control their size and shape and stimulate new buds for next spring.
- [ ] If rainfall is sparse, mulch newly planted trees and shrubs and water them deeply when the soil beneath the mulch feels dry. Unmulched plants will need watering every few days.
- [ ] Prune diseased or damaged branches from trees promptly. Make smooth cuts, leaving the branch collar to facilitate healing. In case of disease, disinfect tools by dipping them in hot water mixed with household bleach.
- [ ] Watch for and pull off dangling bagworm cases on needled evergreens.

Warm Climates

- [ ] Deadhead faded flowers to groom plants and stimulate rebloom later in the season. Allow self-sowers to retain their last blooms.
- [ ] Check soil moisture frequently if rainfall is sparse. Regularly water newly planted perennials.
- [ ] Spread a 2- to 3-inch layer of organic mulch, such as chopped leaves or pine needles, over bare soil between plants to discourage weeds, keep the soil moist, and enrich the soil as it gradually decomposes.
- [ ] Promptly pull any plants that show viral or bacterial disease. Remove the nearby soil as well. Then disinfect tools with a mixture of hot water and household bleach.
- [ ] Fill in bare spots with annuals to provide continuous color during the hottest months.

- [ ] Except in extremely hot inland areas, plant tropical and subtropical trees and shrubs such as hibiscus, gardenia, orchid tree, and palms.
- [ ] Water established trees and shrubs deeply but infrequently to encourage their roots to reach far into the ground.
- [ ] Mulch all plants heavily (but don't pile mulch against their stems) to prevent evaporation of moisture from the soil.
- [ ] Watch for and pull off dangling bagworm cases on needled evergreens.
- [ ] Promptly prune diseased or damaged branches from trees. In cases of fireblight on pear, cotoneaster, cherry, and others, cut branches at least 8 inches below the visible infection. After each cut, disinfect tools by dipping them in hot water mixed with household bleach to avoid spreading the disease.

Annual Flowers

- ☐ Plant seeds for late-summer annuals early in the season.

- ☐ Water containers daily. Include water-soluble fertilizer every week or two if there is no slow-acting fertilizer in the potting mix.

- ☐ Deadhead faded flowers to keep plants compact and neat, stimulate continuous bloom, and prevent self-sowing.

- ☐ Spread a 2- to 3-inch layer of organic mulch over bare soil between plants to discourage weeds and keep the soil moist and enriched.

- ☐ Promptly pull any plants that show viral or bacterial disease such as crown rot. Remove the nearby soil. Then disinfect the tools with a mixture of hot water and household bleach.

- ☐ Routinely inspect foliage for pests. Knock off Japanese beetles into a jar of soapy water.

- ☐ Begin to harvest flowers for drying.

- ☐ Plant a crop of fall-blooming annuals to create lots of color late in the season.

- ☐ Water hanging baskets, windowboxes, and other containers daily. Add fertilizer to the water every week or two if there is no slow-acting fertilizer in the potting mix.

- ☐ As flowers bloom, pick them for drying. Pick herb foliage to dry before plants form flowers.

- ☐ Discourage weeds and keep moisture in the soil by replacing mulch that has decomposed in the heat.

- ☐ Routinely inspect plants for pest problems. Knock Japanese beetles off foliage into a jar of soapy water. Keep the hose handy to spray off aphids and mites from foliage.

Vegetables

- ☐ Harvest cool-weather crops such as peas. Pull out the vines and plant a summer crop.

- ☐ Cover berries and peas with netting as they ripen, to protect the crops from critters.

- ☐ Plan to extend the gardening season into fall. Start seeds for cool-weather crops indoors or in a nursery bed outside about three months prior to the expected first frost.

- ☐ Water when rainfall is sparse. Most plants need about 1 inch of water a week.

- ☐ Remove black plastic mulch or cover it with organic mulch. Cover soil with organic material to moderate temperature and retain moisture.

- ☐ Monitor plants for insect problems and begin controls immediately.

- ☐ Stimulate production of squash, beans, eggplants, and others by picking them when they're young.

- ☐ Water when rainfall is sparse. Most plants need about 1 inch of water a week. Tomatoes like even more moisture.

- ☐ Mulch all bare soil in the garden to prevent evaporation of moisture and discourage weeds. Renew the layer when it decomposes.

- ☐ Monitor plants for insect problems and begin controls immediately.

- ☐ Plant succession crops of beans, carrots, and corn to stagger the harvest.

- ☐ Erect shade cloth over plants to shield them from the afternoon sun, even if they're sun-loving varieties. (They still need some shade in the hottest months.)

fall in the garden

drying flowers

Dried flowers evoke memories of sunny days long after summer is gone. They are a way to keep the garden vibrant and real in your memory during the bleak winter months ahead. You can begin picking and drying flowers as soon as the plants start blossoming. By fall, many blooms you've picked will be thoroughly dried and ready for arranging. Those still growing in the garden will have wonderful seedheads and pods, which make lovely additions to arrangements. ❧Flower drying is as much an art as a science. All kinds of garden and wild plants are good candidates for one or another of the common drying methods. Trial and error will reveal which flowers dry well and hold their color

preserving dried flowers

Spray flowers dried in silica gel with floral spray so they don't reabsorb humidity and droop. Treat air-dried flowers with floral spray or hair spray to prevent them from shattering. Be sure to coat all sides of petals and leaves thoroughly.

❧To show off maximum color and texture of dried flowers, display them in harvest baskets. Freshen and decorate your rooms by mixing lots of different blooms with aromatic dried foliage or scented oils.

❧Dried floral arrangements may be formal or informal. Because dried flowers have less density than their fresh counterparts, you'll need more dried flowers and foliage to fill a display container.

❧Wreaths of dried materials have an ancient history as symbols of friendship and good luck. Use sturdy flowers if you want to mount them on a door.

❧All varieties of rosebuds air-dry well. Wire their stems for support and hang them for at least four weeks. All roses darken in color when dried.

longest. Harvest flowers on a low-humidity day after the dew has dried. Choose those that are nearing their peak and are in perfect condition; discard any that show blemishes and insect damage. Collect enough flowers to allow for losses. Be sure to include as much stem as possible with each one.

❧Try all kinds of flowers, and don't forget wild ones such as Queen-Anne's-lace. The vegetable and herb gardens are treasure troves of possibilities. Flowering trees and shrubs are another. Harvest the blossoms of peegee and oak-leaved hydrangea in stages as they dry on the plants and gradually change color.

the best flowers to dry

Each of these flowers is an excellent candidate for drying. Of course, you'll want to find out which ones grow best in your part of the country.

- Astilbe
- Baby's breath
- Bells of Ireland
- Blazing star
- Celosia (crested or plumed)
- Cosmos
- Feverfew
- Globe amaranth
- Globe thistle
- Goldenrod
- Hydrangea

- Lavender
- Miniature rose
- Ornamental grasses
- Ornamental onion
- Scotch broom
- Statice
- Strawflower
- Thrift
- Yarrow
- Zinnia

flower-drying techniques

❧You can air-dry many flowers outdoors in shade and low humidity or indoors in a dry, warm attic. Hang bunched stems upside down or stand them upright in empty vases.

❧Bury multipetaled flowers such as these marigolds in a box of silica gel or other desiccant powder such as borax. Cover tightly. Check dryness in three weeks. To create a stem, insert florist wire into flower and wrapwith florist tape.

storing the harvest

A bountiful harvest is a joy that more than repays you for the time and energy invested in your garden. For optimal freshness and nutrition, harvest each crop at its peak of ripeness, then promptly use, process, or store it. ❧Some vegetables are fragile or have ephemeral flavor and are best eaten straight out of the garden. Sometimes different varieties of the same vegetable are better keepers, so you'll want to plant those varieties as the fall crop. This information is listed in seed catalogs and on individual seed packets. ❧Store only healthy produce that has been picked when it's fresh and newly ripened. Overripe, damaged, or diseased crops deteriorate rapidly, even if correctly stored. ❧Store

weather

Fall vegetable crops maturing into cooler weather grow more slowly than spring-planted ones that mature into increasingly warm weather. This provides a larger window of opportunity for you to harvest them before they bolt and go to seed or toughen and become woody. Many cool-weather crops withstand—and even benefit—from frost. Some can remain in the garden under mulch almost all winter long.

⤳Harvest pumpkins when they're uniformly orange. If a rap on the side of a likely looking prospect yields a sharp thud, it's ripe. Unless weather threatens, wait until the vines die before harvesting.

⤳Harvest kohlrabi when it is about 2 inches across, before it gets tough. Use your fingernail to test for tenderness, then harvest for two to three weeks.

storing garden vegetables

vegetable name	cool place	in the garden	room temperature
Broccoli	■		
Brussels sprouts	■	■	
Carrots	■	■	
Chile (hot) peppers	■	■	■ (short term, dried)
Collards	■		
Corn	■	■	
Kale	■		
Kohlrabi	■	■	
Leeks	■	■	
Lettuce	■ (dry)		
Onions	■		
Peas	■ (dry)	■	
Potatoes	■	■	
Radishes	■		■ (short term)
Spinach	■	■	
Turnip	■		
Winter squash	■ (dry)		

vegetables properly. Don't wash them until ready to use. For short periods, keep them moist and cool in the refrigerator, dry and cool in a cold room or cellar, or at room temperature. For the long term (several months), process them for freezing, drying, or canning as soon as possible after you've picked them.

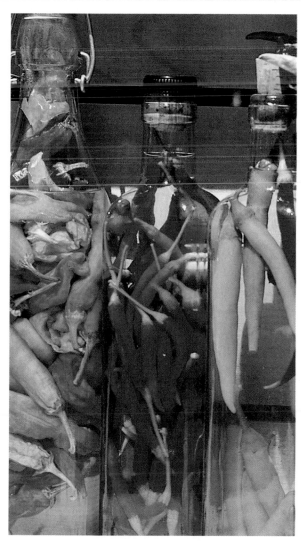

🐌Pick hot peppers throughout the season. They won't get hotter even if you leave them on the plant. Enjoy their heat long after the harvest by preserving their flavors in vinegar or drying them.

making a braid of garlic

1 Harvest garlic bulbs within three weeks after their foliage ripens and collapses. Dig them up—with the foliage still attached—and clip off any overlong roots.

2 Allow the bulbs to air-cure in a dry shady place for a week or two until their skins are crisp and the foliage is dry yet pliable. Starting with the four largest plants, begin to braid the stems.

3 Wrap and weave the garlic stems, incorporating additional stems intermittently. As you proceed, try to graduate from larger bulbs to smaller ones for good proportion.

4 Add new stems so that the garlic bulbs lie progressively along the length of woven braid and don't bunch up at the base. Plan on a medium-length braid, rather than an overlong one.

5 Fasten the top of the braid securely with florist wire or a rubber band. Tie a bow or knot of decorative string that also can serve as a loop for hanging the braid. Although the kitchen is the logical place for display, garlic stores best in somewhat dry, cool conditions away from direct sun. Softneck garlic braids better than the hardneck variety and can keep for four to six months.

planting fall perennials

Fall is a wonderful time for planting. Though it's not the traditional planting season, it should be. In fact, it's an ideal time for lots of plants, including many trees and shrubs, to be moved from one place to another. Divide and replant perennials, set out hardy bulbs that will bloom in spring, and introduce new plants into your yard. Fall-planted perennials benefit from the increasingly cooler temperatures as they adjust to their new surroundings. Their roots don't have to support burgeoning leaf growth and cope with hot, possibly dry weather while they're trying to get established. About the only plants that don't do well are fall bloomers. Theoretically you can plant

planting oriental poppies

YOU WILL NEED

- trowel
- organic matter
- slow-acting fertilizer
- Oriental poppy roots
- water

weather

Alternating freezes and thaws during the winter disturb soil. Sometimes they cause it to heave newly planted bulbs and rooted plant crowns to the soil surface. Always mulch planting beds with 3 to 4 inches of organic material.

1 Dig planting holes slightly larger than each poppy root and 2 to 3 inches deep. Space holes a foot or more apart. Mix organic matter and granular, slow-acting fertilizer into the soil.

2 Plant dormant Oriental poppy roots in late summer to early fall. Divide established plantings to thin clumps or to increase the supply of plants. Oriental poppies like well-drained soil.

3 Spread the roots at the bottom of the hole, the knobby crown facing upward so that any foliage is above soil level. Fill the hole with soil; water well.

4 Firm the soil around the plant crown by hand and water again to rinse off any foliage. Mulch the bed with chopped leaves or evergreen boughs.

most container-grown items anytime during the season. However, goldenrod, chrysanthemums, and asters do best if planted in spring so their roots are well established by the time they produce their flowers. ❧Unfortunately in fall you won't be able to find as wide a choice of perennials in garden centers as you will in spring. The plants you do find may be severely root-bound after being confined in a pot all summer long. However, if properly handled, they should do just fine—and they may be on sale. If you live in an area where the ground doesn't freeze hard until November, perennials that

after the poppy blooms fade

Oriental poppies do a disappearing act after they bloom in late spring and early summer. Their leaves melt away as the plants go dormant to escape the heat. Plant annuals —or place planted containers—in the vacated area. Remove them in early fall when fresh, new poppy foliage reappears in anticipation of next year's bloom.

planting fall perennials (cont'd.)

you plant just after Labor Day will have plenty of time to make themselves at home. ¶Whatever the time of year, thorough soil preparation and the proper planting techniques are the keys to healthy perennials. Dig the soil to aerate it, and remove weeds, stones, and other debris. Take this opportunity to improve the soil's texture and water-holding capacity by digging in some organic matter such as peat moss, compost, leaf mold, or similar material. This also will improve drainage. Delay fertilizing until next spring if the soil is decent. When new growth starts in spring, sprinkle some granular, slow-acting fertilizer on the soil so the spring rains can soak it in. The food will provide consistent, uniform nutrition over several weeks while the

safety first

When working with stone, always wear protective clothing—gloves, sturdy boots, and long sleeves and pants. When you do any lifting, be sure to bend your knees to protect your back.

rodent alert

Rodents, such as mice and chipmunks, often nest in and around stone walls. Their activities disturb the soil behind the wall and may dislodge plants. Inspect plants often to be sure that they're secure in the wall and are getting sufficient moisture.

planting perennials along a path

1 Be sure the plants you place in or near paths are low-growing and sturdy so they'll withstand errant footsteps. The gravel base under stone walks provides good drainage for herbs and minor bulbs.

2 Create planting pockets by leaving generous spaces between stones or by removing existing stones or bricks from an established walkway. Dig holes deep enough to accommodate the root balls.

3 Set the root ball in the hole at or slightly above the surface of neighboring stones. Fill the hole with soil, and water the plant well.

4 Prune all stems that intrude onto the walking area. Water again to rinse the stones and thoroughly moisten the soil.

plants push rapid new growth. Plant perennials at exactly the depth at which they were in their pots—never deeper. As you remove each plant from its pot, check the roots. If the roots are wrapped in circles, pry them loose or make vertical cuts through them to encourage growth to the sides.

Set each plant in its hole, firm the soil over its root ball and around its stem, then add water. Water the plants every five to eight days, particularly when the soil feels dry. Mulch with 2 to 3 inches of chopped leaves, wood chips, pine needles, or compost to insulate the soil over the long winter.

plants for tough spaces

These plants are especially appropriate for planting in walls or paths:

- *Ajuga*
- *Corsican mint*
- *Creeping sedum*
- *Dianthus (pinks)*
- *Golden moneywort*
- *Johnny-jump-ups*
- *Lamb's ears*
- *Portulaca*
- *Serbian bellflower*
- *Soapwort*
- *Sweet alyssum*
- *Thyme (creeping and woolly)*

99

planting a stone wall

1 Insert plants on the face of a dry stone wall—one with no mortar between the stones—by creating planting pockets. Temporarily remove a stone or eliminate a portion of it to open up a space.

2 If possible, scoop out soil to make a hole. Otherwise pack soil into an empty crevice between stones. Most rockgarden plants have shallow, fine root systems and don't need much soil.

3 Position the plant and fill in around its roots with soil. Pack soil tightly around plants inserted into wall crevices. Wedge in small stones if necessary.

4 Snugly fit a stone against the new plant to hold it in place. Water thoroughly. The plant will receive moisture through spaces between stones.

dividing perennials

There are at least four good reasons to divide perennial plants. One is to maintain their health and vigor, because overcrowding stresses plants. When crowded, their dense foliage doesn't dry out after morning dew or rainfall. This, in turn, invites fungal disease, which thrives on poor air circulation around the plants. Stressed plants also invite insect infestations, which only add to the problems. As some perennials age, the center of the clump may become woody and unproductive. And the soil around the plant may have been depleted of nutrients from years of inattention. A second reason to divide plants is to maintain their beauty and peak flower production. Aged and overcrowded plants

YOU WILL NEED

- daylilies
- shovel
- water
- sharp knife or hatchet
- organic mulch

weather

In many parts of the country, fall is a somewhat rainy season. At that time, cool temperatures reduce a plant's need for moisture. However, if rainfall is sparse, be sure to water transplants regularly. Fall-divided plants need consistent water to spur root growth before the soil freezes.

digging and dividing daylilies

1 Dig up the clump of daylilies to be divided by inserting the shovel deep into the soil around the perimeter to loosen roots and isolate the clump.

2 Force the shovel under the root ball and lever the ball up and down to loosen and position it on the shovel. Then lift the shovel and root ball.

4 Spray the soil off the root ball. Then identify individual plant crowns with one or more "fans" of leaves and lots of roots emerging from the base.

5 Pry or cut apart individual crowns. Roots of older clumps may be so tough and tangled that you'll need to chop them with a hatchet.

have small flowers and sparse, small leaves. They're root-bound so they don't take up nutrients efficiently from the soil. The result is faded flower and foliage color and often stunted stem growth. ❧Third, when you divide and replant, you also control excessive spread. Enthusiastic growers, such as yarrow and artemisia, need dividing every year or two. ❧Finally, by dividing plants, you make more plants. And most perennials, other than those with taproots, can be divided easily. When you cut off rooted sections from the root balls of existing plants, you automatically have instant new plants, rooted

3 Shake or brush the excess soil from the root ball. Don't worry if you break a few roots along the way. Daylilies are tough.

6 Replant the divisions promptly so the roots don't dry out. Plant at the same depth as before and water well. Cover the soil with mulch.

dividing perennials

plant name	when to divide	how often
Artemisia	spring or fall	1–2 years
Astilbe	spring	1–3 years
Baptisia	spring or fall	10 or more
Bee balm	spring or fall	2–3 years
Black-eyed Susan	spring or fall	4–5 years
Boltonia	spring or fall	4–5 years
Chrysanthemum	spring or fall	3–5 years
Coreopsis	spring or fall	1–3 years
Daylily	anytime	4–5 years
Daylily, rebloomer	spring or fall	2–3 years
Epimedium	early spring	6–10 years
Garden phlox	spring	1–3 years
Goldenrod	spring or fall	4–5 years
Hellebore	spring	10 or more
Hosta	spring or fall	10 or more
Hypericum	spring or fall	1–3 years
Lady's mantle	spring or fall	6–10 years
Ornamental grass	spring	3–4 years
Peony	late summer	10 or more
Sedum 'Autumn Joy'	early spring	6–10 years
Veronica, spike	spring or fall	1–3 years
Yarrow	spring or fall	1–2 years

dividing perennials (cont'd.)

and ready to grow. They're exact replicas of the originals, sharing their desirable characteristics and growth habits. And they're free. ❧ Divide your perennials either in spring or fall when heat or frozen ground isn't a factor. Wait until a plant clump is large, so the loss of chunks of its roots won't undermine its health. If your goal is to obtain more plants, do your dividing in early spring. Because they're just beginning to emerge from dormancy and send up small

shoots, the plants won't be shocked much by the process. The roots have been resting all winter and aren't yet required to support major growth. The obvious exceptions are those plants that bloom in spring. Wait to divide bleeding heart, barrenwort, pulmonaria, and others until they've finished

YOU WILL NEED

- shovel
- trowel, sharp knife, or spade
- compost
- water
- organic mulch

weather

Divide plants late in the day or when the sky is overcast. Protection from the sun will spare them additional stress during the process and once they're replanted. If rain is expected, plant just before it's due.

digging and dividing hostas

1 Spring is the best time to divide hostas, but you also can do it in fall after they bloom. Dig around and under the clump to loosen the roots.

2 Lift the root ball out of the ground. Use a trowel, sharp knife, or spade to cut between leaf stems and through the roots to separate chunks of plant.

4 Tuck hosta divisions into shady beds around the property or in their own bed. Enrich the soil with compost so it holds moisture and drains well.

5 Plant each division at the same depth as before. Firm the soil over the root zone. In fall, hosta foliage is mature and will soon die back with frost.

blooming. Spring division gives transplants plenty of time to become established. ◥However, if your goal is to improve plant health or control spread, divide in fall—unless the plants are fall bloomers. Cut back their stems and dig them up. If the center of the plant is old and woody, cut rooted sections from healthier outer portions of the clump and discard the spent center part of the root ball. If plant roots are badly matted or have bulged toward the soil surface, make sure each division has roots by teasing them apart and cutting down through the plant crown.

3 Isolate individual plants or small groups of plants. To minimize stress, make sure that each section has some leaves and lots of roots.

6 Water newly planted hosta divisions well. Spread a 2- to 3-inch layer of organic mulch over the soil to insulate it for the winter.

digging and dividing chrysanthemums

1 Hardy mums bloom from late summer to mid-November in many parts of the country. Divide them after they bloom; some late bloomers can be divided in spring. Cut off dried flower stems back to the leaves.

2 You can divide mums in place, if you wish, simply by digging a section out of an existing planting and removing it, then refilling the hole with soil. An alternative, of course, is to dig up the entire clump, then divide it.

3 Shake the soil from the roots, then cut down through the stems and leaves into the woody crown to create separate plants. Be sure each division has plenty of roots.

4 Replant new divisions as soon as possible. Keep them well watered throughout autumn if rainfall is sparse. Mulch them with chopped leaves or other organic matter to insulate the soil.

planting bulbs

Spring-flowering (or hardy) bulbs are the ultimate low-maintenance flowers. Because their roots can withstand winter cold and frozen soil, they rebloom year after year. And they emerge on schedule every spring without any fuss, long before you've begun your traditional gardening chores. A little fertilizer once a year and mulch over the soil keeps them happy. All plants in the bulb category share an interesting trait—modified structures that store starch, which provides the energy to fuel their growth and flowering. Whether these structures are called bulbs, corms, tuberous roots, or rhizomes, they function the same way. After the plants flower, their leaves continue to soak up sunshine for several

YOU WILL NEED

- spading fork
- organic material
- bulb fertilizer
- garden rake
- bulbs
- trowel or bulb planter
- water
- mulch

selecting bulbs

Buy only top-quality bulbs for the best performance. Look for large, firm bulbs with smooth, unblemished surfaces. They're well worth the slightly extra expense.

mass planting

1 Good soil preparation provides the drainage that hardy bulbs require. Use a spading fork to dig down at least 12 inches in the soil to loosen and aerate it, so the bulb roots will grow deep.

2 Mix in organic material, such as compost, leaf mold, or peat moss, to enrich the soil and improve its ability to hold moisture. If your soil is heavy clay, consider building a raised bed.

4 To create an informal, natural-looking planting area, scatter the bulbs randomly. If necessary, adjust them slightly to maintain reasonable spacing.

5 Use a trowel or bulb planter to dig individual holes roughly twice as deep as the height of the bulb. Set each bulb in the hole, pointed tip upward.

weeks. This builds energy reserves from nutrients that are taken up by the roots and stored in the bulb. Their job completed, the leaves ripen, yellow, and collapse. Hardy bulbs rest beneath the soil, escaping summer heat until next season. ▼The best time to plant bulbs is in early fall, when cool weather

bulb-planting tools and tips

A hand trowel is an ideal tool for planting bulbs in clusters. Excavate flat-bottomed holes that are large enough to accommodate several bulbs. Odd-numbered clusters look best.

Use a bulb planter or an auger attached to a power drill to dig lots of individual holes over a large area. This makes it easier to plant bulbs in drift patterns.

A minishovel or a long-handled trowel works well for planting small bulbs. Insert it into the soil to the desired depth. Press it forward to open a crevice, then drop in the bulb.

Although narcissus are poisonous to animals, many other bulbs are tasty. Plant them in wire cages to protect them. Their roots can grow easily through the wire into the soil below.

3 Mix in granular, slow-acting fertilizer that's specifically formulated for bulbs. Then rake the area smooth, removing any stones, weeds, and other debris you find.

6 Fill each hole with soil and firm it gently over the bulb. If rain isn't expected soon, water the bed to settle the soil. Cover the area with mulch.

planting bulbs (cont'd.)

prompts them to come out of their dormancy. There are many kinds of hardy, spring-blooming bulbs. Some of the earliest bloomers are snowdrops, crocus, squill, and winter aconite, which brave the winter cold to carpet the ground with color as early as February in some regions. Tuck them into the soil at the front of the garden, under trees and shrubs, along walks, or even in the lawn. They multiply and spread by forming tiny bulblets. Use them to form large patches or clusters so they're very visible. ◥Tulips, daffodils, and wonderfully fragrant hyacinths are favorites for spring. Different varieties of each bloom early, midseason, or late to provide a steady parade of color. You can use them, too, for cut flowers, so plant lots of them. Because daffodils are poisonous

tender bulbs

Gladiolus, canna, dahlia, caladium, tuberous begonia, and other summer-blooming bulbs are called tender bulbs. Because their roots can't handle frozen ground, plant them in spring for summer bloom if you live where winters are cold. In Zone 8 and warmer, you don't have to dig up tender bulbs in fall—they can stay in the ground year-round.

planting tulip beds

1 Plant beds of tulips or other hardy bulbs all at once rather than one bulb at a time. Create your layout by placing the bulbs on top of the soil, then moving them around to make the pattern you want.

2 Dig one large hole about 6 inches deep in the designated planting area and mix in organic matter to create good texture and drainage. Then sprinkle some bulb fertilizer on the soil.

5 Firm the soil over the entire area to ensure good contact with the bulbs. Add more soil if the level of the bed sinks below the surrounding ground.

6 Add water if you expect no rain. Use a gentle, deep-soaking spray, which won't disturb the bulbs. The moisture signals them to begin growing roots.

to critters, plantings in wooded areas survive for years. They still get the necessary sun, because they bloom and die back before most trees leaf out. Unfortunately deer love tulips, so be sure to plant them where they're protected. Although spring bulbs are relatively carefree, they do need some attention. After they bloom, pinch off the faded flowers. This concentrates the plants' energy toward revitalizing the bulb. Allow the leaves to persist, fully exposed to the sun, until they yellow. Then clean them up to make way for more plants that may be coming up nearby.

bulb-planting time

For the best root growth, plant hardy bulbs in early fall. The smaller the bulb, the sooner you should plant it, because small bulbs tend to dry out easily. However, if you anticipate a delay, store the bulbs temporarily in a dark, cool place. If you should suddenly remember—in the middle of winter—that they're still in the cellar or garage, plant them whenever and wherever the ground isn't frozen, then water and mulch them well.

107

3 Position individual bulbs at the bottom of the hole. Set them in small clusters or randomly (rows look like soldiers). Be sure the flat bottoms contact the soil and the pointed tips face upward.

4 Fill in the hole, covering the bulbs so that they're buried under 4 to 5 inches of soil. In colder climates, tulips are more likely to come back year after year if planted as deep as 8 to 10 inches.

7 Cover the beds with winter mulch by spreading 3 to 4 inches of chopped leaves, shredded bark, or other organic material to insulate the soil.

forcing bulbs indoors

You can bring spring indoors early by forcing bulbs to bloom ahead of schedule. Pot up daffodils, tiny iris, tulips, and crocuses at the same time (or even later, with leftover bulbs) that you plant them outside in fall. Choose varieties recommended for forcing, and select only the largest, firmest bulbs. Set them in a refrigerator or other cool, dark place (ideally just above freezing) for several months, then enjoy their beauty all winter long. The chill time in the refrigerator simulates the onset of spring so the bulbs develop roots. ❧ Plant bulbs in any type of pot with a drainage hole. Broad, shallow containers, called bulb pans, are best because they don't tip over when

YOU WILL NEED

- pot
- soil-less potting mix
- bulbs
- decorative mulch (optional)
- water
- cool, dark storage place

paperwhite narcissus

Paperwhites don't need a chill period, so they can be forced easily. Set bulbs snugly on a layer of gravel in a flat, shallow bowl without a drainage hole. Add water to cover the gravel, and maintain that level at all times. Keep in a sunny window.

forcing tulips

1 Choose a pot that is at least twice as deep as the bulbs to allow for proper root growth. Be sure it has a drainage hole. Fill it about half full of soil-less potting mix.

2 Set bulbs barely touching, with their growing tips even with or just below the pot rim. A 6-inch pot will hold up to six tulips, three daffodils, or 15 minor bulbs such as crocus or grape hyacinths.

4 Water the pot well, then place it in a refrigerator or in a cool, dark room where the temperature will remain between 33° and 50°F.

5 Check the moisture level every few weeks. When shoots begin to show, take the pot out into a bright, warm room so the bulbs will grow and bloom.

plants become top-heavy with bloom. Space potted bulbs closer together than those in the garden. For a lush, thick show, try growing two layers of different bulbs in a deep container. Plant one type of bulb, cover it with soil, then position the other bulbs between the growing points of those already buried.

3 Cover the bulbs with potting mix so the tips are just showing. You may want to add a thin mulch of attractive gravel or moss, though this optional step is strictly cosmetic.

bulbs you can force easily indoors

plant name	weeks chilled
Crocus	10–14 weeks
Daffodil	16–22 weeks
Grape hyacinth	12-16 weeks
Hyacinth	10–14 weeks
Paperwhite narcissus	no chill
Snowdrop	10–14 weeks
Tulip	14–20 weeks

winterizing roses

Roses are so beautiful that it's difficult to begrudge them the extra attention they require over the growing season. As cool fall weather brings on their dormant period, one final job remains for you: preparing them for winter. As a group, hybrid tea roses are the most vulnerable to winter cold and need the most preparation. The complexity of this job depends on how severe the winters typically are in your part of the country. ❧It's important to stop fertilizing in late summer in most areas. Make the last feeding of the season two months before you expect the first frost. Also refrain from major pruning, and stop cutting blossoms. This avoids stimulating any more new, tender growth, which will be killed by the first frost anyway. ❧Remove all old mulch from under and around the roses; it might harbor insect eggs or disease spores from infected fallen leaves. Just before the first hard, or killing, frost of the season, spread fresh mulch of wood chips, shredded bark, or chopped leaves around the base of the plant, extending as far out as the branch tips. Wait until

YOU WILL NEED

- stakes
- burlap
- string
- organic mulch

getting tree roses ready for winter

1 Tree roses, or standards, are vulnerable to the cold, so you'll want to help them cope with winter. Begin by setting four stakes in the ground around and just beyond the mulched root zone.

2 Wrap a protective barrier of burlap around the stakes and tie it in place with string. Then fill in the middle with an insulating layer of shredded dry leaves. The rose is now shielded from harsh winds.

weather

Spring weather is fickle. Delay removing mulch until leaf buds swell. Keep polyspun garden fabric handy to cover exposed roses if frost threatens after you've removed the winter mulch.

cold-hardy hybrid tea roses

- **'Chicago Peace'** – pinkish double flowers turning apricot at their base
- **'Chrysler Imperial'** – deep red double flowers and spicy fragrance
- **'Double Delight'** – cream-tinged with red, becoming redder with maturity; extremely fragrant
- **'Garden Party'** – double-flowered with pink-tinged white petals
- **'Mister Lincoln'** – velvety, dark red double flowers; highly fragrant
- **'Pascali'** – scented white flowers
- **'Perfect Moment™'** – double flowers, red with yellow bases
- **'Tiffany'** – scented, pink double flowers
- **'Tropicana'** – brilliant orange flowers and fruity fragrance; also a climbing form
- **'White Delight'** – double flowers, ivory with pink centers

after the ground freezes to spread the mulch if rodents are a problem in the yard. Mice, especially, like to build their nests in mulch. Water the rose well, especially if it's been through a dry summer. ❧ Once the ground freezes, it's time to add more mulch. If you live in an area with relatively mild winters, simply mound the mulch over the plant crown 6 to 12 inches up the canes. This insulates the soil to maintain an even temperature in spite of the normal alternating winter freezes and thaws. This thick mulch is especially important when there is no reliable snow cover to protect plants. If winter temperatures often drop well below zero, build the mound of mulch, then add more material after every freeze to make the mound higher. Eventually the mulch should virtually cover the bush. Sometimes it's easier to enclose the shrub in a cylinder and fill it with mulch.

cold-hardy roses

To minimize winter rose care, choose varieties that are reputed to withstand cold temperatures. Landscape (shrub) roses, old garden types, and miniatures are quite hardy. Hybrid teas and grandifloras generally require the most care, although certain varieties are hardier than others. Look for roses grown on their own roots rather than grafted ones if hardiness is a concern.

111

protecting roses with mulch

🌿Enclose shrubs in cylinders of cardboard, metal, or plastic or in commercially made foam rose cones for maximum protection. Fill them with shredded bark, paper, or leaves for added insulation.

🌿Protect the graft (or bud union) and crown of roses by mulching with loose soil, wood chips, shredded bark, or shredded leaves. Mound the mulch to a foot high over the base of the plant.

🌿The canes of climbing roses are vulnerable to winter wind and sun. They need special attention in regions where winter temperatures typically drop below zero. Either wrap the canes with burlap or detach them from their supporting trellis and lay them horizontally on the ground. Cover them with a mulch of leaves, wood chips, or soil.

making leaf mold

Leaves are a valuable natural resource. Rather than regard them as a nuisance, be grateful that the trees on your property drop a new supply of them every fall. It takes very little effort on your part to recycle them into a wonderful soil conditioner— leaf mold—for the yard and garden. Unlike compost, leaf mold is only partially decomposed, leaving bits and pieces of the leaves visible in the finished product. And, again unlike compost, leaf mold is derived only from leaves. ❧You can make leaf mold the same way nature creates it on the forest floor. Just pile up moist leaves and wait for them to decompose. If you want to speed up the process, you can shred the leaves into smaller pieces before piling them up. Enclose the pile, if you wish, with snow fencing, chicken wire, or something similar to improve its appearance. Make sure the container allows air to circulate, because oxygen fuels the decomposition process. Over the winter, the pile will shrink as decay reduces the volume of leaves—a sign that the process is well under way.

YOU WILL NEED

- turkey wire or hardware cloth
- tall stakes (optional)
- sledge hammer (optional)
- leaf rake
- mulching mower
- compost fork
- wheelbarrow or garden cart

1 Set up a wire cylinder or similar container to hold the accumulated leaves you'll be collecting. (It will help keep the wind from blowing the leaves around.) If necessary, add stakes for stability.

2 Rake up leaves as soon as possible after they fall. The job will be easier if you gather small amounts frequently, rather than rake a large accumulation all at once. It also prevents matting and lawn damage.

Leaf mold helps build healthy soil in several ways. When mixed into poor soil, it improves its texture. The coarse organic material creates air spaces in the soil, making it easier for roots to penetrate. Leaf mold also improves the soil's ability to absorb moisture and keep it available longer for plant roots. As the leaves continue to decompose, they improve the soil's fertility by creating a population of active microbes. Leaves are a favorite food of earthworms, which convert the leaves into nutrient-rich castings that are distributed throughout the soil. Spread leaf mold on top of bare soil as an organic mulch. It keeps the soil from being compacted by hard rains and drying sunshine. And it helps the soil retain moisture by decreasing evaporation, absorbing rain, and reducing wasteful runoff. Leaf mold gradually breaks down in the heat of summer, so renew the mulch layer whenever it becomes thin.

discouraging weeds

Leaf mold mulch does an effective job of discouraging weeds if you remove existing weeds from the area first. Spread a thick layer of leaf mold to block the sun from seeds that remain in the soil. The layer can be thinner in shaded areas where weeds are less bothersome. And it should be no deeper than 3 or 4 inches over tree roots.

113

3 The smaller the pieces of organic material, the faster they decompose. Shred leaves by mowing the lawn where they lie with a mulching mower, then raking. Or rake them into a pile and mow over it.

4 Load the shredded leaves into the cylinder. (Those that are damp will decompose faster.) Don't compress the leaves in the container, because good airflow promotes decomposition.

5 When spring comes around, the leaves in the center of the pile will be fairly decomposed and those on the outside less so. As you transfer the leaves to a wheelbarrow or cart, be sure to mix the various layers together before you spread them.

winterizing garden tools

Quality tools deserve quality care. And tools that are in top condition make your work easier and time spent shorter. A sharp spade slices through a tough clump of tangled roots in practically one motion. Sharp pruner blades cut through branches cleanly, minimizing the possibility of disease and further damage. Sharp lawn mower blades cut grass cleanly, preventing excess moisture loss through frayed foliage tips. ❧Every month or so take a few minutes to smooth off nicks or gouges on tool edges before they become worse. Carefully file the bevel to maintain an edge. Clean the dirt from tools after each use. Use a wooden stick to wipe or scrape off shovels and rakes; the wood won't scratch

keeping tools clean

An effective way to clean dirt from the metal parts of shovels, spades, and digging forks is to shove them into a 5-gallon pail of sharp builder's sand saturated with used oil from your car, lawn mower, or other gasoline-powered equipment. Move the metal part of the tools in and out of the sand several times to scour and rustproof them for winter storage.

❧If you use a moistened whetstone to sharpen a shovel, be sure to maintain the same angle of bevel. To smooth out nicks, make repeated strokes the length of the whetstone along the entire shovel edge.

❧When you use a file to sharpen a shovel, hold the file at a 20- to 30- degree angle to the blade edge. With a smooth motion and medium pressure, stroke the length of the file across the cutting surface.

❧To sharpen loppers with a moistened whetstone, stroke across the upper of the two bypass blades, following the established angle.

❧If you use a file to sharpen loppers, make several gentle passes along the upper, sharpened, blade of the two bypass blades.

the metal, so rust is avoided. Remove dried clippings that cake under the mower. Put tools away after each use. At season's end, rub wooden handles with linseed oil and replace those that are split. Oil metal blades to prevent rust. Replace worn blades on pruners and mowers. Store everything in a dry place.

Sharpen a hoe with a file just as you do a shovel. Stroke the length of the file at medium pressure across the hoe edge. Try for a clean bevel rather than a knife-sharp edge.

Sharpen shears with a moistened whetstone by stroking the cutting edges of the blades. Be sure to move across the bevel at the same angle.

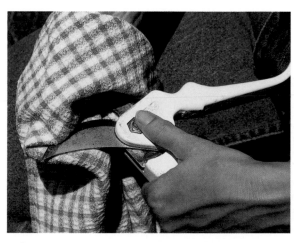

Regularly wipe cutting blades of pruners, loppers, and hedge shears with a cloth to maintain their edge as long as possible between sharpenings.

putting the garden to bed

Putting the garden to bed for the winter is mostly a matter of cleaning up and covering up. As fall progresses and temperatures drop, those plants that aren't killed outright by frost prepare for dormancy. Clear out the blackened stems and foliage of annual flowers and vegetables to prevent the possibility of their harboring disease pathogens and insect eggs over the winter. The cool weather is a good time to make a cold frame, dig and box in raised beds, and make general repairs. While it appears as if all activity in the garden has stopped, there's a lot going on under the soil until it freezes. Newly transplanted trees and shrubs, divisions of perennials, and hardy bulbs are all growing roots,

weather

Snow both protects and endangers plants. A good snow cover insulates the soil like a mulch. However, snow piled on evergreen branches weights them down, risking breakage. Knock snow from the bottom branches first, then work upward. This way snow from above will not add weight to the already burdened lower branches. If branches are bowed by ice, don't try to free them. Instead let the ice melt and release them gradually.

protecting plants

Cut back dry stems of perennials to soil level after frost to neaten the garden and remove pest eggs and disease spores that may linger. Leave stems with attractive seed heads for winter interest.

Compost dead plant debris to create an organic soil conditioner. Hot, active piles kill weed seeds and disease pathogens; passive, inactive piles do not. Throw questionable plant material in the trash.

Cut off diseased foliage from evergreen plants and shrubs and discard it in the trash. Rake up and discard the old, disease-bearing mulch, too.

To prevent rodents from nesting in the soil, wait until the ground freezes before adding a 6-inch layer of organic material as winter mulch.

drawing on soil nutrients and moisture around them. Earthworms and various microbes in the soil are still processing the organic material they're finding. Most likely, the organic mulch you spread to protect the soil during the summer months has substantially decomposed. It's important to spread new mulch now —a thicker winter layer—to protect plants and soil over the winter months. The idea is not so much to keep the soil warm as it is to keep the temperature even. Once the soil is frozen, mulch keeps it frozen. So if you have shade trees, convert the fallen leaves to mulch and use it throughout your property.

Mulch perennial and shrub beds with pine needles or chopped leaves. This protects both plant roots and the soil and moderates the effects of extreme temperature changes during winter freezes and thaws.

Mulch bulb beds with evergreen boughs to protect the soil from shifting and cracking during the winter. Otherwise plants, especially small, shallowly planted bulbs, can be heaved to the surface.

Protect the tender bark of young trees from gnawing critters by wrapping stems or trunks with wire or commercial tree-guard products.

Screen evergreens, particularly exposed broad-leaved types, from drying winter wind and sun by setting up burlap screens or shade cloth shelters.

regional fall checklist

	Perennials	**Trees and Shrubs**

Cool Climates

Perennials
- ☐ Divide spring- and summer-blooming plants.
- ☐ Plant new perennials, especially those that bloom in spring.
- ☐ Set up a compost bin for fallen leaves and garden debris. Put diseased plant material in the trash.
- ☐ After the ground freezes, spread a winter mulch over any bare soil in the garden. Spread evergreen boughs over bulb beds.
- ☐ Clean and sharpen garden tools; store in dry place.
- ☐ After frost, clean up perennial beds and borders. Cut down dead flower stems. Dig up and discard any weeds and diseased plants.
- ☐ Build a cold frame to overwinter marginally hardy perennials and provide a chill period for bulbs being forced for winter bloom.
- ☐ Dig up tender bulbs such as dahlia, canna, and gladiolus. Wrap or cover them with moist material and store in a cool, dark space.

Trees and Shrubs
- ☐ Transplant shrubs or young trees to new locations on the property in early fall.
- ☐ If rainfall is sparse, deeply water trees and shrubs—especially evergreens—before the ground freezes.
- ☐ After the ground freezes, spread a winter mulch—up to 6 inches thick—of organic material such as chopped leaves.
- ☐ Fertilize young trees and shrubs that have been in the ground for at least a year. There's no need to fertilize old, established trees and shrubs, especially if they're mulched.
- ☐ Winterize roses by mounding mulch over the lower parts of their canes. In cold regions, shelter them with a burlap screen.
- ☐ Take down and clean out birdhouses. Make repairs over the winter.

Warm Climates

Perennials
- ☐ Continue checking plants for pest infestations and disease outbreaks. Identify and deal with any factors that may be stressing the affected plants and making them vulnerable to these problems.
- ☐ Clean up perennial beds and borders. Cut down dead flower stems. Dig up and remove diseased plants. Weed areas that weren't mulched.
- ☐ Divide overlarge clumps of spring- and summer-blooming plants to control their size and renew their blooming.
- ☐ Dig new beds and renovate existing ones. Plant new perennials and transplant others.
- ☐ Plant cool-weather annuals such as pansies.

Trees and Shrubs
- ☐ Water citrus and avocado trees well to prevent the fruit from splitting.
- ☐ Disbud camellias for larger blooms. Water camellias regularly to prevent buds from browning and dropping off. Mulch with pine needles.
- ☐ Stop feeding tropical trees and shrubs in September to give them time to harden off for winter dormancy.
- ☐ Plant or transplant nontropical trees and shrubs around the property. Delay fertilizing until spring.
- ☐ Prune injured branches from trees and shrubs.
- ☐ Take down and clean out birdhouses. Make repairs over the winter.

Annual Flowers

- ☐ Keep polyspun garden fabric handy to cover annuals when light frost threatens.

- ☐ Collect seeds of favorite plants that will breed true to type.

- ☐ Take cuttings of geraniums, coleus, impatiens, and begonias to root for houseplants.

- ☐ After a killing frost, pull up dead annuals and put them on the compost pile. Discard in the trash any that have fungal disease.

- ☐ Clean, sharpen, and store garden tools in a dry place for the winter.

- ☐ Mulch annual beds with a 3- to 4-inch layer of chopped leaves or similar material. If you're expecting self-sown seeds to germinate next spring, spread the mulch only 2 inches thick.

- ☐ Make notes or save labels of favorite annuals to remember them for next spring.

- ☐ Plant seeds of cold-hardy annuals for extended winter bloom. Collect seeds of favorite warm-weather plants that will breed true to type.

- ☐ Keep polyspun garden fabric handy to cover annuals if light frost threatens.

- ☐ Take cuttings of geraniums, coleus, impatiens, and begonias to root for houseplants.

- ☐ Continue to weed, water, and watch for pests. Renew organic mulch in areas where it has decomposed and thinned in the heat of summer.

Vegetables

- ☐ Keep polyspun garden fabric handy to cover summer crops such as beans and peppers if an early light frost threatens.

- ☐ Harvest crops such as pumpkins, potatoes, sweet potatoes, and onions. Brussels sprouts, carrots, and other root crops can stay in the ground through light frosts.

- ☐ Clean up plant debris in harvested beds. Mulch or sow cover crops on empty beds to protect the soil over the winter.

- ☐ Beds where root crops will be stored in the ground over the winter need to be mulched with thick layers of straw or chopped leaves.

- ☐ Tend fall crops such as broccoli, cabbage, spinach, and onions until they're mature and ready for harvest.

- ☐ Harvest green tomatoes and store them indoors.

- ☐ Build more boxed raised beds. Repair trellises. Clean out cold frames.

- ☐ Renew beds for fall planting by adding more organic matter such as compost and fertilizer.

- ☐ Sow carrots, beets, and other root crops as well as lettuce for fall harvest.

- ☐ Set out cole crop transplants such as cauliflower, Chinese greens, cabbage, broccoli, and mustard. Shade them if the days are still warm.

- ☐ Clean up plant debris in harvested beds. Mulch or sow cover crops on empty beds to protect the soil over the winter.

- ☐ Build more boxed raised beds. Repair trellises.

119

winter in the garden

amaryllis & paperwhites

The sight of blooming bulbs in winter, even if indoors, is indeed a promise of spring. In chapter four, you learned how to force hardy bulbs to bloom indoors out of season. That is a somewhat long-term project because of the chill period needed to get the bulbs growing. Other bulbs, such as amaryllis and paper-white narcissus, are native to warmer parts of the world and don't require the chill of winter to begin growing and blooming. ❧ Both types of bulbs are sold from mid-September until the end of December. Often they're preplanted in pots and available as kits, which make good gifts. Both amaryllis and paperwhites take only six to eight weeks to bloom, compared to a

growing amaryllis

good lighting

Stems of amaryllis and other bulbs tend to lean toward the source of their light. If they're on a sunny windowsill, turn them a bit every day to encourage them to develop straight stems. If the light source is above them, as with fluorescent units, the stems will be straighter. Continue to adjust the fluorescent light so it remains within 6 to 8 inches of the buds at the stem tips as they grow. This will keep the plants shorter and more compact.

❧ Soak amaryllis bulbs in water just before you plant them. Set each dormant bulb in a snug pot that has a drainage hole and is filled with potting mix. Bury the bulb in the mix, leaving its top one-third exposed. Keep the mix moist but not soggy, and set the pot in a sunny spot until the buds open. As the rapidly growing stalk elongates and bears four or five blooms, it may need support.

minimum of 12 to 14 weeks typical of forced bulbs such as crocus, tulips, and hyacinths. Buy and start amaryllis and paperwhites in fall so they'll bloom for the year-end holidays. The bulbs you buy at holiday time will flower for Valentine's Day. Store the bulbs dry at room temperature until you're ready to plant them. Don't wait too long before you pot them up, because they may start sprouting in their packages. Once they're planted, watered, and blooming, keep them in a cool room to prolong their beauty. They don't need direct sun once their buds are open, but give them lots of bright light.

growing paperwhites

Fill a 3- to 4-inch-deep container without drainage holes two-thirds full of pebbles. Position the bulbs on them, shoulders touching, with points up. Surround the bulbs with pebbles and add water just to their bottoms. Set the container in a cool, dark room for three weeks while the roots grow. Move it to a sunny, cool room to develop green shoots and buds. Expect flowers in about 10 days.

common forcing mistakes

There are at least five good reasons why forced-bulb projects may fail:

■ **Improper storage of bulbs awaiting planting can cause irreparable harm.** Temperatures that are too high will kill the flower buds, although the vegetative buds that produce leaves may not die. If you delay the planting process for some reason, the bulbs may dry out.

■ **Temperatures during the chill stage can be too low for too long.** Prolonged exposure to subzero temperatures will kill even tough crocuses and tulips. Ideally, temperatures should gradually drop as they would outdoors, settling at 33 to 45 degrees F. A refrigerator does just fine.

■ **Bulbs can receive too little or too much water.** Potted bulbs need to be damp but not soggy. If you allow them to get too dry, they'll abort their flowers. Cover them with plastic, or water them periodically, especially if you're chilling them in a frost-free refrigerator, which removes moisture.

■ **The transition from winter storage to the hot, dry indoors (winter to spring) can be too abrupt.** Sudden exposure to bright sun after many weeks in the dark may stunt their growth or shrivel new buds. Gradually move potted bulbs toward a sunny window.

■ **Too little light can cause pale, limp leaves and stems.** At their normal bloom time outdoors, the daylight hours are increasing. Indoors in winter, bulbs need a sunny window and possibly help from a fluorescent light.

pruning fruit trees

Fruit trees are both ornamental and productive, so annual pruning is doubly beneficial. The best time to do major pruning is late winter or early spring, because you're stimulating rapid growth of new stems. Leaves haven't emerged yet, so the branch layout is clearly visible. ▼Yearly pruning establishes, then maintains, the shape you want. The *central leader system* is common primarily for ornamental fruit trees. Prune to establish a single leader, or trunk, then encourage lateral branches at regular intervals around it. The *modified leader system* features a central leader and three or four equally important major branches. Cut away all other large branches. Use the *open center system* for orchard

pole pruners

Long-handled pole pruners are ideal for clipping thin upper branches from the canopy of a small tree. They allow overhead work without the nuisance and danger of a ladder. Look for models tipped with small saws or cord-operated, crook-shaped cutting blades. Pole pruner handles extend up to 8 feet.

Remove root suckers that sprout from the base of the tree—they actually come from its roots—as soon as they appear. Use loppers to cut them off as close to the base as possible.

Water sprouts are suckers that grow vertically from tree limbs. Because they divert valuable energy from the fruit-bearing branches, immediately clip them off cleanly with your loppers.

Use a pruning saw to remove large branches that are injured or rubbing a neighbor. Make the first cut upward, several inches out from the trunk.

Make the second cut at the trunk but leave the branch collar—the ring of transition bark at the crotch—to grow callus tissue, which heals the wound.

trees. Prune to encourage three or four major limbs instead of a central trunk. The limbs should angle out widely and support six secondary, fruit-bearing branches each. This flattened shape opens the canopy to air, and the lower profile makes the fruit more accessible. ❡Always prune bottom to top, inside to outside, and remove any dead or damaged wood. If two branches are rubbing together, cut off the poorer-positioned one all the way back to the trunk or main limb. Encourage branches that grow upward and outward from the tree's center or that fill an opening in the overall profile of the tree.

rejuvenating an apple tree

Apple trees live a long time. It's possible to restore a venerable tree that has been neglected for years by carefully pruning it over several seasons. First determine that it doesn't have any trunk rot or root rot that has compromised its basic health. Then clear away brush and prune back neighboring trees that shade it. Cut off suckers and twiggy growth throughout the branch canopy to let in sunlight. Each year afterward, prune away only one-fourth to one-third of the new growth so you can control suckering. Water and fertilize the tree.

125

pruning evergreens

Most evergreens have neat, symmetrical habits and don't require much pruning. Some, such as eastern white pine, are brittle and suffer damage in rain- or snowstorms. Cleanly prune away injured branches to avoid more damage from disease or pests. Otherwise prune evergreens just to maintain symmetry and encourage denser foliage. Stimulate the development of more twigs by cutting individual branch tips with shears or clippers.

❧Some conifers—cone-bearing, needled evergreens—branch out randomly and sprout new growth wherever latent buds appear. Arborvitae, hemlock, and yew—good hedge material—respond well to aggressive shearing by producing dense, new

YOU WILL NEED

- gloves
- hand pruners or hedge shears
- debris container
- household bleach
- hot water

avoiding browned tips

To prevent temporary browning on cut ends of needled evergreens, prune them when they're wet. Choose a time just after a spring rain or early in the morning when the dew is heavy.

pruning for size

1 Cut back branches of broad-leaved evergreens, such as holly, with hedge shears to encourage denser growth. Create a more natural look by cutting individual stems with hand pruners .

2 Use pruners or loppers to clip off dead and injured branches as soon as you discover them. Cut back to where fresh foliage occurs or where the branch joins the trunk.

3 Prune to guide the natural growth of each shrub. If you need to do heavy pruning each year to control its growth, it's the wrong plant for the space.

4 Clean up all debris afterward. If there are signs of disease, bag trimmings in plastic for the trash. Disinfect tools with household bleach and hot water.

foliage. ❧Other conifers, such as pine, juniper, fir, and spruce, branch out differently. All their main branches grow directly from their trunks, radiating outward like spokes of a wheel. Simply trim branch tips. They won't grow new foliage if pruned back too far. ❧Don't constantly prune a shrub to keep it squeezed into a space that's too small for it, because you'll stress and disfigure it. If it's too large for the space, move it to a place that can handle its mature size. Choose cultivars that will mature to the size of your space. You'll find many dwarf conifers these days that are just right for small yards and gardens.

pruning for shape

1 Make cuts to maintain a shrub's natural shape. Clip the individual stems of needled evergreens when their soft "candles" of new growth appear in late winter. Cut back each candle by about one-half.

2 Replace a shrub's central leader if it breaks or fails to develop. Select a nearby stem and bend it upward, fastening it if necessary so it's dominant.

common pruning errors

Incorrect pruning mars appearance, undermines vigor, and compromises health—good reasons to avoid these errors:

- **Topping –** Cutting off the top of a tree forces it to develop new, weaker, multiple replacement stems. It will struggle to achieve its genetically programmed height.

- **Heading back –** To shorten a branch, cut where another branch or side twig emerges rather than at just any point along the way.

- **Cutting back stems to bare wood –** Many shrubs don't generate new twigs and foliage from branches (those usually near the trunk) that have no leaves or twigs already.

- **Shearing into tight shapes –** Except for certain shrubs that easily withstand shearing for hedges, repeated shearing promotes dead twigs and foliage loss inside the shrub.

- **Leaving a stub –** Cleanly cut off branches at the trunk and leave only the branch collar to heal into a small nob.

forcing branches to bloom

Force flowering trees and shrubs to bloom prematurely by bringing a few cut branches inside and giving them an early spring. Because most plants need a dormant period of rest and cold, wait until early February to do your cutting. The length of the cold spell they need varies by plant variety, but this timing works for most. Choose plants with many new flower buds formed just after last year's bloom. Flower buds are typically plumper than leaf buds, which are usually slim and pointy and lie nearer the stem. The closer to their normal bloom time, the faster the branches will bloom indoors. So cut early bloomers, such as spirea, forsythia, witch-hazel, fragrant honeysuckle, quince,

YOU WILL NEED

- hand pruners
- pail
- tepid water
- floral preservative or chlorine bleach
- display container

branches for form and berries

Many shrubs and trees have interesting shapes or colorful berries that can be cut and added to flower arrangements or displayed on their own. Some possibilities include firethorn, Harry Lauder's walking stick, beautyberry, viburnum, corkscrew willow, and winterberry holly.

1 Your goal is not only to cut a branch to force inside but also to preserve the natural shape of the shrub or tree and ensure a good outdoor bloom display later. Cut branches with lots of plump buds.

2 Ensure maximum water uptake by recutting the stem ends at a sharp angle to expose as much surface to the water as possible. Clean off buds from the part of the stem that will be underwater.

3 Promptly put the cut stems in a pail of tepid water with commercial floral preservative —or a drop of chlorine bleach—to fight bacteria.

4 Set the pail in a cool place for a week or two. Change the water periodically if necessary. When buds begin to swell, bring it into warmth and light.

and wintersweet, in early February. Cut later bloomers —crab apple, cherry, azalea, rhododendron, flowering dogwood, and redbud—in early to mid-March. Cut branches during the warmest part of a mild day, when buds have the most sap. Allow them to adjust indoors for a week or two. Pamper them with moisture.

5 Rearrange the stems in fresh water and floral preservative in the container of your choice for display. Set it in bright light but not sunlight. The warmer the room, the faster the buds will open. However, for longer display life, you'll want to keep them in a cool area. Once they've bloomed, as in the above photo, you have a miniature version of your outdoor plant that can bring spring's beauty indoors well ahead of its normal arrival.

other plants you can force

Callery pear bears small, musky-scented white flowers in rounded clusters with emerging leaves. Cut in mid-March for bloom in two to three weeks.

Cherry trees bear clusters of pink flowers. If cut in mid-February, earliest varieties bloom indoors in two weeks, the later ones in three to four weeks.

Redbud bears pealike purplish-pink (sometimes pink or white) flowers along bare branches. Cut branches in March for indoor bloom in three weeks.

Apple blossoms start as clusters of deep pink buds. They open to 1-inch, dainty, scented white flowers with emerging leaves. Cut stems in March.

Flowering quince is forced indoors easily in January to early February. It bears 1½-inch-wide red, pink, orange, or white flowers on spiny stems.

Forsythia bears 2-inch-long, trumpet-shaped yellow florets along its arching branches. If cut in early February, it will bloom indoors in two weeks.

pruning roses

You can enjoy incomparable blossoms from your hybrid tea roses all summer long if you prune them back—a step that's probably harder on you than on the plant. No matter how difficult it is on you to cut back each bush to a few small, short canes (stems), it's essential to the rose's health and well-being. Hybrid teas and their close relatives, grandiflora and floribunda roses, respond to annual, early-season pruning with vigorous new growth. When you remove winter-killed wood, excess canes, and rubbing branches, you groom the plants and shape their growth so they stay relatively compact in size and produce lots of flowers. Without this care, the bushes typically become tall and rangy

YOU WILL NEED

- heavy gloves
- hand pruners
- loppers (optional)
- pruning saw (optional)

foiling fungus

The foliage of many hybrid tea roses is vulnerable to fungal disease. Prune it down to outward-facing leaves to maintain good air circulation in the center of the shrub. This is the first line of defense. Mulch plants well to prevent rain from splashing spores up onto foliage.

1 In late winter just as leaf buds begin to swell, prune hybrid tea, grandiflora, and floribunda roses. Remove all deadwood, then stimulate growth by cutting back healthy canes (stems) to 6 inches.

2 Make clean, slanting cuts about ¼ inch above a leaf bud that faces outward. This encourages outward growth and keeps the center of the plant open for good air circulation.

3 Remove any canes that crisscross. The goal is three or four healthy canes on a hybrid tea bush. Remove all others, stubs and all.

4 A properly pruned rose looks small and vulnerable. However, it will grow properly in just a few weeks and produce beautiful blossoms.

and produce fewer, smaller flowers. ❧Prune roses with the correct equipment. Sharp bypass pruners will handle most of the cutting. Use long-handled loppers—also with bypass blades which won't crush the stems—or a pruning saw for extra-thick canes, and old and neglected bushes or in situations where thorns on nearby stems make access difficult. ❧Remove any part of the shrub that's brown and brittle, which, after a severe winter, may amount to a great deal. Entire canes may be brown to their base, and part of the crown at the soil level may be dead. Just remember: Pruning is doing the plant a favor.

pruning roses in bloom

Cutting rose blossoms for indoor display is a form of pruning. Take care to prune each stem back to where its leaves are composed of at least five or more leaflets. Cut on a slant just above an outward-facing leaf. Use the same technique to remove any faded blossoms on the shrub. This promotes a neat, compact shape and grooms the plant.

131

roses that need minimal pruning

Roses with the shrub or landscape designation don't require much pruning. Although they respond to shaping and look better when the dead stems are cut away, their habits are less formal:

- Rugosa hybrids
- Flower Carpet™ roses (pink, white, and appleblossom)
- 'Caretree' roses (Carefree Beauty™, 'Carefree Wonder', Carefree Delight™)
- 'The Fairy'
- Meidiland hybrids (Bonica™ and others)

better late than never

Prune roses about the time that forsythia begins to show its yellow buds. However, sometimes you may find it impossible to prune on schedule. Fortunately it's never too late to thin stems from the center and cut away deadwood. In fact as the shrub leafs out, you can tell right away which canes need removal. Just prune away all of the dead brown parts.

regional winter checklist

Cool Climates

Perennials

- [ ] Spread winter mulch over perennial beds after the ground freezes hard.
- [ ] If the ground hasn't frozen yet, finish planting any bulbs that were overlooked during the fall.
- [ ] Take a soil test if the ground is still workable.
- [ ] Make a list of perennials that will need dividing in spring.
- [ ] Have the lawn mower blade sharpened.
- [ ] Catch up on unread issues of gardening books and magazines that have been lying around.

Trees and Shrubs

- [ ] Erect a screen of burlap, shade cloth, or similar material (never plastic) to protect broad-leaved evergreens exposed to drying winter winds.
- [ ] Brush heavy snow off evergreen boughs to keep them from breaking. Start with the lower branches, then work upward.
- [ ] Spray foliage of broad-leaved evergreens with antidesiccant to help them retain moisture.
- [ ] Allow the ice on branches to melt on its own.
- [ ] Prune away the ragged stubs of broken and injured branches promptly with a smooth cut just in front of the branch collar.
- [ ] Mound mulch or soil over the crown and partway up the canes of hybrid tea roses.
- [ ] Prune large shade trees while they're dormant and the branch architecture is visible.
- [ ] Spray fruit trees with dormant oil before leaf buds swell.

Warm Climates

- [ ] Protect perennials from heavy frost by covering them with a bedsheet, polyspun garden fabric, or a makeshift tent of plastic (with ventilation holes).
- [ ] Mulch bulb and perennial beds to insulate the soil from temperature fluctuations.
- [ ] Catch up on unread issues of gardening books and magazines that have been lying around.

- [ ] Prune and spray fruit trees, other deciduous trees prone to problems, and hybrid tea roses with dormant oil prior to leaf bud break. If leaves are out, use light (superior) oil.
- [ ] If frost threatens, shelter tender shrubs with polyspun garden fabric, or a bedsheet.
- [ ] Plant bare-root trees and shrubs and transplant any others to new sites.
- [ ] Promptly prune any injured or broken branches from trees and shrubs.
- [ ] Buy and plant sasanqua camellias while they're in bloom.
- [ ] Cut branches from early-flowering shrubs and trees and bring them indoors for early bloom.

Annual Flowers

☐ Look through mail-order catalogs to select annual seeds you can start indoors during late winter. Try something new.

☐ Get out seed-starting equipment and order peat pots and other supplies.

Vegetables

☐ After a hard frost, clean up dead, dried plant debris. Cover beds with several inches of straw or chopped leaves, or plant a cover crop to protect the soil.

☐ Mulch beds where root crops such as carrots and parsnips remain to protect them until they're all harvested.

☐ Look through mail-order seed catalogs and order seeds in time to start cool-weather crops indoors.

☐ In late winter, prepare one bed for planting cool-weather crops.

☐ Get out seed-starting equipment and order peat pots and other supplies.

☐ Build new compost bins or repair old ones. Turn and consolidate compost piles to prepare for the new season.

☐ Get out seed-starting equipment and order peat pots and other supplies.

☐ Deadhead and maintain the area around cool-season annuals such as pansies.

☐ Look through mail-order seed catalogs and order seeds in time to start cool-weather crops indoors.

☐ Continue to enjoy lettuce and Chinese greens by protecting them in a cold frame or with polyspun garden fabric or a plastic tunnel.

☐ Get out seed-starting equipment and order peat pots and other supplies.

☐ Build new compost bins or repair old ones. Turn and consolidate compost piles to prepare for the new season.

gardening basics

climate

Plants grow most successfully if adapted to the climate where they're planted. Based on measurements of the lowest recorded temperatures across the country, the United States Department of Agriculture (USDA) has designated a series of geographic climate zones. They're numbered from 1 to 11, coldest to warmest. ❧Check plant tags when buying perennials so you know whether they will tolerate winter in your zone (or a colder one). The tags usually list a hardiness range. If they list only one zone, it's generally the coldest area where the plant will survive. Local nurseries and garden centers usually stock plants appropriate to local climate conditions. ❧Then there are the microclimates on your property—those conditions that vary over just a few yards. Areas near the house, which provides shelter and radiates heat, are warmer than slopes exposed to harsh wind and sun. Be aware of these variations when siting your plants.

USDA hardiness zone map

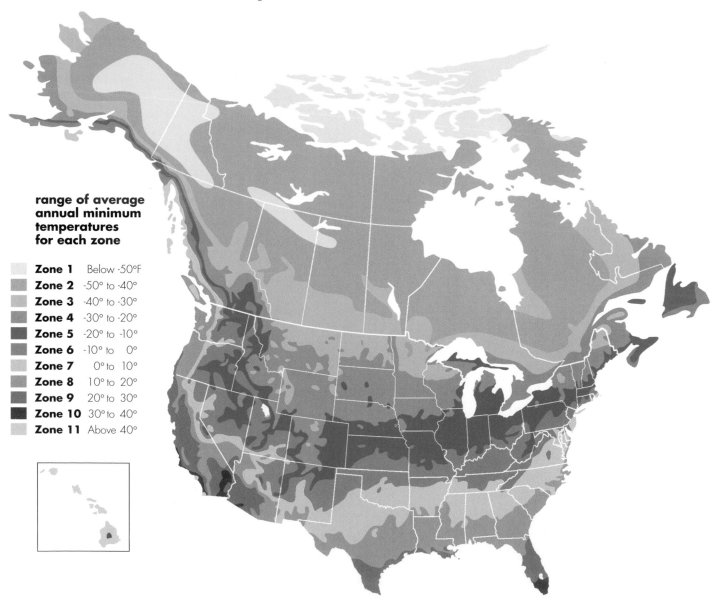

range of average annual minimum temperatures for each zone

	Zone 1	Below -50°F
	Zone 2	-50° to -40°
	Zone 3	-40° to -30°
	Zone 4	-30° to -20°
	Zone 5	-20° to -10°
	Zone 6	-10° to 0°
	Zone 7	0° to 10°
	Zone 8	10° to 20°
	Zone 9	20° to 30°
	Zone 10	30° to 40°
	Zone 11	Above 40°

spring frost dates

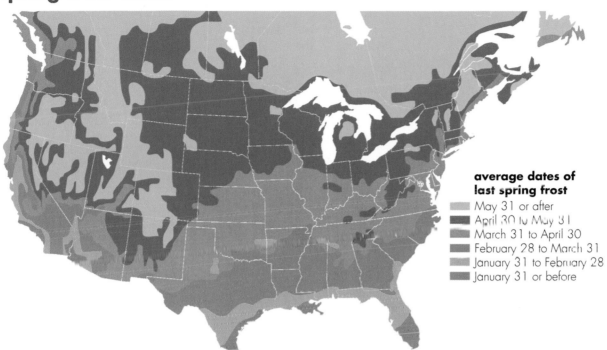

**average dates of
last spring frost**

May 31 or after
April 30 to May 31
March 31 to April 30
February 28 to March 31
January 31 to February 28
January 31 or before

fall frost dates

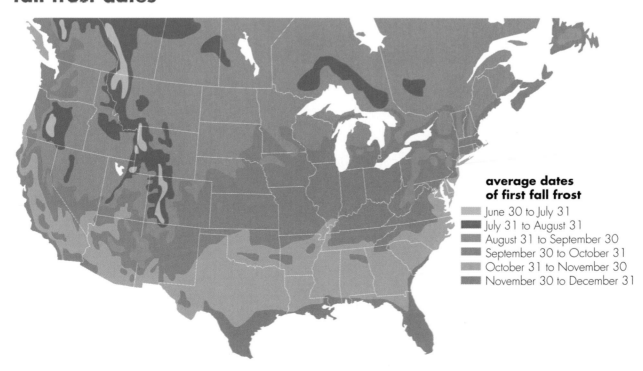

**average dates
of first fall frost**

June 30 to July 31
July 31 to August 31
August 31 to September 30
September 30 to October 31
October 31 to November 30
November 30 to December 31

basic gardening tools

There's no denying that gardening is hard physical work. But it's *pleasurable* hard work, made all the easier by good-quality, appropriate tools. Choose quality over quantity. A few basic tools, well designed for comfort and carefully crafted of the best materials, will serve in most situations. If you care for them properly, they should last a lifetime. ⬩Today's tools are ergonomically designed to spare backs, shoulders, and wrists. Space-age materials make them lighter, more balanced, and easier to grip and use without developing calluses. Choose those that are well-manufactured and made of high-grade materials. Look for features such as replaceable parts, holes in

garden spade

A spade is not the same tool as a shovel. It is short-handled and has a flat, squared-off blade. A spade is ideal for edging beds, digging planting holes, slicing under sod, and working soil amendments into the garden. In a pinch you can even use it to chop ice on walks. Its versatility makes it a staple in the toolshed.

garden fork

Dig into the soil with the four sturdy, straight steel tines of a garden fork. Also known as a spading fork, it's a good tool for turning and aerating the soil. Use it to break up big chunks of soil and to work in organic matter, fertilizer, and other amendments. It copes easily with occasional roots or buried rocks and comes in handy for dividing clumps of perennials.

shovel

A garden shovel typically has a dished, or concave, blade that is rounded or mildly tapered at the tip. Most shovels are long-handled, although you can buy them with short handles, too. Because the blade is canted at an angle to the handle for greater leverage, a shovel is ideal for attacking piles of soil, sand, and other materials you need to load or move.

hoe

Cultivate the soil and remove young weeds in a garden bed with a hoe. The simplest hoe is basically a straight-edged, square blade attached at a right angle to a long wooden handle. It's useful for chopping clumps of soil and scraping the soil surface to cut off sprouting weeds. When you tilt the hoe at an angle, you can trace neat planting furrows in prepared soil with the corner of the blade. There are many types of hoes. A swan hoe has a curved neck. A diamond hoe has a head that is diamond-shaped, perfect for weeding between plants.

handles for hanging, and easy-cleaning rustproof metal parts. ❧Try out the tools in the store before taking them home. Check the grip to ensure that it will be comfortable for repeated use. Good pruners, for example, come in different sizes to fit your hand and grip. If you have small hands, you will want a pruner that doesn't open wider than your hand. Handle length is very important as well. A hoe, for example, should come to the middle of your head (nose height). Properly used, it is held upright, and you use a forward and back motion with your hands and forearms only. No bending over or backache.

steel rake

Also called a garden rake, this tool features 12 or 14 short steel tines mounted on a sturdy steel bridge at the end of a long handle. Use this rake to dress and smooth out prepared soil in a planting bed. Its tines simultaneously break up small clods of soil and corral stones and debris. Use a flathead style to level the soil for planting by flipping the rake over so its bridge scrapes along the soil surface.

flexible rake

The business end of this type of rake, sometimes called a lawn or leaf rake, is a fan of flat, flexible tines. Typically bent at their tips, the tines are made of graduated lengths of metal, bamboo, plastic, or even rubber in a variety of styles. The tines are attached to a long handle for easy control. Use a flexible rake to gather light debris that's spread out on beds, lawns, and walkways and to rake up leaves.

trowel

The basic hand tool for digging, a trowel is indispensable for planting bulbs, seedlings, and other small plants in a garden bed. Trowels are available with sturdy handles and narrow or wide cupped metal blades with tapered tips. Different sizes—widths and lengths—suit different planting jobs.

hand weeder

This tool is basically a miniature hoe, and most gardeners use it for down-and-dirty weeding. The short handle at the end of a flat, straight-edged blade allows you to maneuver between plants in a bed. The blade may be square or triangular and mounted at any one of various angles for flexibility. Position the blade on the soil and draw it toward you to cut off weeds at or just below the soil level. Or turn the blade upward so its corner will dig deeper to dislodge stones or pry out larger weeds.

basic gardening tools (cont'd.)

❧Some essential types of gardening equipment are not necessarily perceived as tools. However, they're almost as useful and certainly as labor-saving as tools such as shovels and pruners. Watering equipment, gardening garb, and devices to carry things fall into this category. They make a big difference in efficiency and safety in the yard and garden. Although they may not be used in direct contact with plants in a garden bed or lawn, they contribute indirectly to the beauty and long life of your plants. ❧Although what you wear in the garden is mainly a matter of personal choice, there are two essentials that you should not overlook—sunscreen and a hat. With the incidence of skin cancer on the rise, it's important for gardeners to take skin protection as seriously as beachgoers

gloves

You'll need several pairs of gardening gloves. Choose cloth or leather gloves to protect hands from blisters. Use those coated with nitrile or plastic that have wide gauntlets to protect wrists and forearms from plants with thorns or prickers. Opt for latex gloves to protect hands from soil-borne fungi, which can cause dermatitis. Check fit by making a fist; then feel for finger fit at tips of glove fingers.

watering can

Because water is crucial to the well-being of plants, a watering can is an old standby. Originally made from galvanized metal—and now a variety of materials from brass to plastic—it retains its classic form: a bucketlike reservoir that holds the water, a bowed handle, and a long spout capped with a sprinkler head, or rose. Choose a can that feels balanced when full and holds a generous amount of water without weighing too much.

hose

A hose is indispensable for maintaining plants in any yard or garden larger than a few square feet. At every life stage, plants need water for good health, and a hose at the ready can bridge the periods of scant rainfall. Buy the best hose your budget will allow. Choose a rubber or vinyl hose constructed of several layers of mesh and with sturdy connectors to ensure long life. It will save you many trips carrying a watering can during hot weather.

hose attachments

Nozzles—which used to be made of brass and now come in a variety of materials, sizes, and shapes—control the stream of water coming out of the hose. A watering wand—a long metal tube with a sprinkler head at the tip—converts the hose to a long-distance watering can. Use it to water containers, hanging pots, and beds. The wand should have a shutoff at its connection to the hose to prevent wasting water. Another key tool is a sprinkler that you attach to the hose on the ground. It either oscillates or rotates to deliver water to beds and lawns. The best ones have a timer and adjustments for the width and direction of the stream.

sprayers

Fertilizers, tonics, fungicides, insecticidal soaps, and many other products are water-soluble and most effective if sprayed on plant foliage. Although many are packaged ready-to-use in spray bottles, they're more economical in concentrated form that you mix in water at home. Sprayers that attach to the hose and dilute automatically are convenient. You might want to have a 1- or 2-gallon- capacity pump sprayer for small jobs. Larger backpack units are useful in spraying fertilizer over broader areas such as lawns.

do. You forget when you're gardening how many hours you're exposing sensitive skin to the sun. You probably spend much of your time in the garden looking down, so you need to protect the back of your neck and shoulders. ❧Although you might be tempted to go barefoot in the garden, especially on a hot summer day, you're better off wearing shoes. Nonskid soles keep you from slipping on damp ground. Brightly colored rubber or plastic garden clogs are catching on for good reason. You can slip them on over bare feet to work in the garden, then step out of them onto any clean floor.

pruners

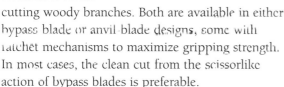

Hand pruners and long-handled loppers are essential tools for cutting woody branches. Both are available in either bypass blade or anvil-blade designs, some with ratchet mechanisms to maximize gripping strength. In most cases, the clean cut from the scissorlike action of bypass blades is preferable.

Use loppers for branches over ½ inch thick. Their long handles require two hands to operate but offer greater leverage.

wheelbarrows, carts, wagons

Yards and gardens generate a lot of debris that you'll need to transport to the compost pile. They also benefit from the loads of organic matter and mulch you haul in and distribute over the area. Garden carts and wheelbarrows do these jobs and many others. Use a stable, two-wheeled cart with high sides for large, bulky loads. It can handle up to 500 pounds on its pneumatic tires. The smaller, nimbler wheelbarrow—now available in one- or two-wheel models—is easier to maneuver into restricted spaces.

pruning saw

Large tree or shrub limbs—anything over 2 inches in diameter—are best cut off with a pruning saw. Bow-type models with straight blades handle the largest limbs and allow you to use a two-handed grip. The compact folding types have curved blades. The more comfortable grips and pointed open blades of these small saws are particularly useful in tight places where there's little space to insert the cutting edge between branches.

141

kneelers and seats

Although one of the many attractions of gardening is the opportunity to kneel down close to the soil, getting up gracefully afterward can become a problem as age takes its toll on your knees and back. Kneelers of various kinds cushion the contact with the hard ground. Those that have a metal frame with tall side bars also help you stand up afterward. Low gardening seats— either on metal frames or on wheeled tool carts—help avoid back and knee strain.

assessing the soil

The relative acidity or alkalinity of the soil—its chemical environment—affects the availability of the nitrogen, phosphorus, and potassium for the plants. And the plants' ability to take full advantage of the nutrients in the soil depends on how well their chemical environment suits them. Some plants, such as azalea and holly, need soil that's on the acidic side. Others need the soil to be sweeter—more alkaline. The soil's degree of acidity or alkalinity is referred to as its pH. Soil pH is expressed on a scale of 1.0 (acid) to 14.0 (alkaline), with pH 7.0 being neutral. ⬦In certain regions of the country, soils are typically more acid or more alkaline. To a great extent, this affects the

soil pH testing

YOU WILL NEED

- pH test kit
- trowel
- soil

1 Fill tube from a pH test kit with soil taken 3 to 4 inches below the soil surface in the test area. Don't touch the soil with your hands. Remove grass, stone, and debris, then crumble the soil finely.

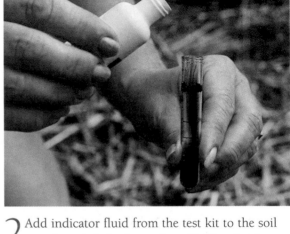

2 Add indicator fluid from the test kit to the soil sample and shake it to mix well. Then let the entire mixture settle. Allow the color to develop for about one minute before you take a reading.

3 Complete the soil test by comparing the color of the solution in the tube with the color chart on the product packaging.

pH preferences of plants

alkaline soil
- Baby's breath
- Black locust
- Cactus
- Clematis
- Lilac
- Onion
- Peony

acid soil
- Blueberry
- Camellia
- Holly
- Hydrangea
- Rhododendron

neutral soil
- Lawn grass

choice of plants suitable for a particular area. For the lowest maintenance, choose plants that prefer a soil pH in the range that prevails in your area. ❧Sometimes conditions cause changes in soil pH. A soil test—done by you, a local nursery, or your county Cooperative Extension Service—will alert you to pH problems. You may have to adjust the soil pH slightly to accommodate certain plants. For instance, most lawn grasses prefer mildly acidic-to-neutral soil. In areas where more acidic soil is the norm, homeowners routinely sweeten the soil by spreading granular or dolomitic lime on it.

fertile soil

🐛Fertile soil has earthworms, which thrive in the organic matter. Their presence indicates soil that also supports microorganisms that process soil nutrients. Earthworm castings add to soil fertility.

🐛Good-grade loam has an ideal texture. It's rich and crumbly and has organic matter, which helps it retain moisture and drain well.

is a pH test necessary?

As useful as it is, a pH test isn't always necessary. The pH needs of most garden plants tend to fall into the mildly to moderately acid range. Because moderately acid soil predominates over large areas of North America, soil pH readings aren't necessary for selecting landscape plants. Trees, shrubs, and perennial plants that are native to an area are already adapted to the prevailing pH. This is one reason why native plants are so highly regarded. Throughout the country, local nurseries and garden centers carry plants that are appropriate to the soil conditions in their region. You also can find out which plants thrive in your area by noting successful gardens in the neighborhood.

There are times when being able to measure the soil's pH is helpful, such as when moving to a new property where there are few existing plants or when considering whether to grow a certain crop in the vegetable garden. Also, nearby construction may alter soil pH. Soil that you'd expect to be on the acid side might suddenly turn alkaline because of lime that leaches from masonry mortar. This happens in established beds along walls and foundations. Plants are the best indicator of pH consistency in soil. As long as they're healthy, the soil is fine. A sudden change in an established plant—for example, hydrangea flowers blooming pink instead of blue—signals pH problems. Sometimes plant leaves turn pale, their dark green veins etched in visible detail. This condition—chlorosis—indicates that the plants aren't getting enough iron, most likely because their soil is not acid enough. In these cases testing the pH confirms that the problems are caused by altered soil acidity.

143

adding organic matter

The key to growing healthy, vital plants is healthy, vital soil. Yet because it's easy for us to take soil for granted, it's also easy to forget how fundamentally important it is. The result: Soils in most residential landscapes are neglected and in poor condition. An important lesson in gardening and yard care is that we must restore and maintain soil so it can provide essential air, moisture, and nutrition to lawns and gardens, trees, and shrubs. ❧Almost half the volume of healthy soil is mineral particles from pulverized rock and flecks of organic material. The other half is equal amounts of air spaces and moisture between these particles. Typically most of the organic material is concentrated in the top 8 to 12 inches, especially in the top 3 inches. Here the topsoil is dark and spongy and filled with teeming populations of organisms processing nutrients for plant roots and neutralizing potentially problematic fungal spores, bacteria, and viruses. ❧Poor soil lacks rich topsoil. Builders often remove it from a site when they begin construction, then fail to replace it

YOU WILL NEED

- garden gloves
- well-rotted (aged) manure, leaf mold, peat moss, or other organic matter
- spading fork

soil cover-up

Protect healthy soil from being compacted and depleted of organic material by covering it where it's exposed to weather. Spread an organic mulch or plant a groundcover on all bare soil to deflect heat, harsh sun, heavy rains, and weed seeds.

1 Composted animal manure is a good source of organic material that you can add to soil. It supplies major nutrients, lively microorganisms, and helpful enzymes. Buy it in bags at garden centers.

2 Canadian sphagnum peat moss absorbs and holds moisture extremely well. Mildly acid, it has coarse organic fibers that condition all types of soil and improve its texture.

adequately at the end of the job. Moreover their heavy equipment, followed by years of foot traffic and kids' play, compacts the remaining soil, which forces most of the air out of it. As a result, moisture has difficulty penetrating it, the soil lacks life and fertility, and the only plants that can cope in it are weeds. ¶Organic material can be your biggest problem solver. When you dig it into compacted soil, the fibrous material loosens the soil's texture and restores spaces to hold air and moisture. It also creates an environment that supports living organisms, from the tiniest microbe to the largest earthworm. As they eat and reproduce, they spur decomposition of the carbon and nitrogen in the organic material and break down rock particles into minerals. Routinely add organic matter to the soil to sustain this activity and build healthy topsoil that's capable of nurturing and protecting plants.

replenishing the soil

Plan to replenish the soil with organic matter every year. It constantly breaks down—especially quickly in hot regions—due to the activity of lively organisms. In established perennial beds where plants generally stay put, mulch between them with compost or leaf mold. Dig some into the soil every chance you get, particularly when you divide and transplant and when you plant annuals among the perennials.

145

3 Use a spading fork to dig organic matter into the soil. Distribute the matter throughout the entire area down to a level of 8 to 10 inches, where most of the plant roots grow.

amending the soil

Amending the soil means adding materials to improve its fertility, texture, or moisture-holding capacity. Most often the prescription for deficient soil is a generous amount of organic material. However, some organic materials are more suitable for certain soil problems than others. Although all are derived from living sources—composed mainly of carbon and nitrogen—they vary in their specific contributions to soil. Some are more effective with sandy rather than clay soil. Others excel at providing nutrients to soil but only marginally improve its texture. ❧Organic matter of any kind improves soil.

Materials that are free and readily available obviously are always the most desirable. That's why compost is so touted: It's free and easy to make in your own backyard, no matter how large or small it is (see pages 154–155). ❧Choose specific amendments to target particular problems. For instance, if the soil lacks humus, which is necessary to support microbial life and earthworms, dig in generous amounts of leaf mold. If the soil is

what amendments do for the soil

	adds volume	improves soil texture	aerates	improves drainage	holds water
ORGANIC					
Canadian sphagnum peat moss	■	■	■		■
commercial potting mix	■	■	■	■	■
compost	■	■	■	■	■
ground bark or sawdust	■	■	■		
humus	■	■	■	■	■
leaf mold	■	■	■	■	■
manure	■	■		■	
mushroom soil	■	■	■	■	■
seaweed (kelp)		■		■	
INORGANIC					
gypsum		■	■		
sand (builder's)			■	■	
vermiculite			■	■	■
water-absorbing polymer crystals (hydrogels)	■				■

compacted, is thin and sandy, or not acidic enough, dig Canadian sphagnum peat moss into the soil. It holds moisture and is slightly acidic. Although there has been a lot of talk over the past decade about the ecological implications of using peat moss in the garden, the bottom line is that the harvesting of peat in Canada does not impact the environment. The peat bogs are vast and the amount harvested is minimal—taken only from the top layer. At the same time as the harvest, the bog is reseeded. The greater issue is the transportation of the resource to various parts of the country. Look for local amendments that you can add to the soil. Inorganic amendments are derived from minerals or other nonliving materials. They, too, play a role in improving soil by supplying basic nutrients and increasing the soil's moisture and air-holding capacity.

feed the soil

Nourish the soil with organic matter anytime the soil isn't frozen. Organic matter offers immediate benefits. Fall is a particularly good time to add both organic and inorganic amendments. Top-dress the lawn with topsoil, compost, or chopped leaves from the mulching mower. Dig organic material into beds, and mulch around shrubs and trees.

147

adds nutrients	special considerations
	Acidifies soil.
■	"Soil-less" mixes have no nutrients.
■	May have antifungal properties.
	Avoid sawdust from pressure-treated wood.
■	Helps feed any soil.
■	The smaller the pieces, the faster the decomposition.
■	Choose aged manure to avoid burning the plants.
	Use only on lawns and ornamentals in case pesticide residues are present.
■	Wash off salt; don't use in clay soil.
■	Conditions clay soil.
	Use coarsest sand possible.
	Use with sandy or silty soil.
	Ideal for containers.

using fertilizers

Fertilizer, rather than plant food, is the true source of soil nourishment. It's designed to supplement the nutrients that occur naturally in soil, enabling it to produce healthy and productive plants. The key to choosing the right fertilizer is understanding the nature of the soil on your property. The less fertile it is, the more fertilizer is necessary. Even if your soil is well aerated and contains some organic matter, it's safe to assume you'll need to add fertilizer. That's because residential landscapes are not only typically planted more intensively than are natural areas, they also contain plants and lawns that are big feeders. ▼Over the years many garden plants tend to use up soil

weather

Temperature affects the rate at which organic fertilizers release nutrients into the soil. Because this release is a function of microbial activity in the soil, these nutrients are more available to plants in hot weather, when soil microbes are most numerous and active. Coincidently this also is the time when plants are growing most actively and need a nutritional boost.

foliar feeding

1 Mix liquid or powdered water-soluble fertilizer with tepid water at half the strength listed on the product label. Stir thoroughly. Spray plant foliage when the temperature is below 80°F.

2 Use a watering can—or hand or pump sprayer—to moisten leaves thoroughly. Cover all surfaces of as much foliage as possible. The fertilizer won't harm blossoms or fruits.

Hose-end sprayers are the most efficient way to foliar-feed large gardens and lawns. Measure the fertilizer into the jar, then attach it to the hose.

N-P-K: what it means

- Plants require three major nutrients: nitrogen (N), phosphorus (P), and potassium (K).

- **Nitrogen** fuels leaf and stem growth. It's the most quickly depleted nutrient.

- **Phosphorus** stimulates root growth and seed formation. It's in greater proportion in fertilizers sold for use in fall, a time of major root growth.

- **Potassium** promotes flowering, fruiting, and disease resistance.

- The proportions of NPK are indicated on fertilizer packages by three numbers, such as 5-10-5. Manufacturers alter the ratios for specific categories of plants, such as roses, vegetables, evergreens, and lawns.

nutrients faster than natural processes can replace them. Fertilizer compensates for the loss. If your soil is more deficient in some nutrients than others, special fertilizer products redress the balance. In cases where soil is compacted and low in organic matter, a complete slow-acting fertilizer will sustain it until you can aerate it and add organic material.

Although plants take up nutrients mostly from the soil, they can also absorb them in liquid form directly through their leaves. Water-soluble fertilizers deliver nutrients rapidly for the short term, but they must be used repeatedly throughout the season.

using granular, slow-acting fertilizer

1 Use granular, slow-acting fertilizer in spring to provide uniform, consistent nutrition over most of the season. Scratch the soil around existing plants, being careful not to harm shallow plant roots.

2 Sprinkle the granular fertilizer on the roughened soil in the amounts suggested on the package label. Water it in or allow the rain to soak the area thoroughly. Then cover with mulch.

3 Dig the granular fertilizer into the top 10 inches of the soil of a new bed. Add it to the potting mix for container plants before planting.

organic fertilizer

- Nutrients in granular, slow-acting fertilizers may be derived from natural sources or synthesized in a laboratory. Both provide exactly the same nutrition, but it's released to plants from the soil by different mechanisms. The nutrients in synthetics are coated to slow down the rate at which they're released when in contact with soil moisture. Those in natural, or organic, products are released by the activity of microorganisms that live in the soil and convert nutrients into a form that plant roots can absorb.
- Organic fertilizers are formulated from a wide variety of natural materials—animal manures, fish meal, rock phosphate, seaweed, wood ashes, seed hulls—that supply nitrogen, phosphorus, and potassium.

reading a plant tag

The plastic label or tag on a purchased plant contains valuable information. Even plants that you buy from mail-order and Internet sources come with plant tags. Occasionally a tag has only the common and/or botanical name—usually at small nurseries that start their own plants from seeds or cuttings. But more and more nurseries and other plant providers rely on large wholesalers to supply them with plants, which come with preprinted plant labels. ❧Some tags are more complete than others. They can provide all the information you need to grow the plant, including its preferences for light and water and its ultimate height and spread. The tag gives a good description

perennials

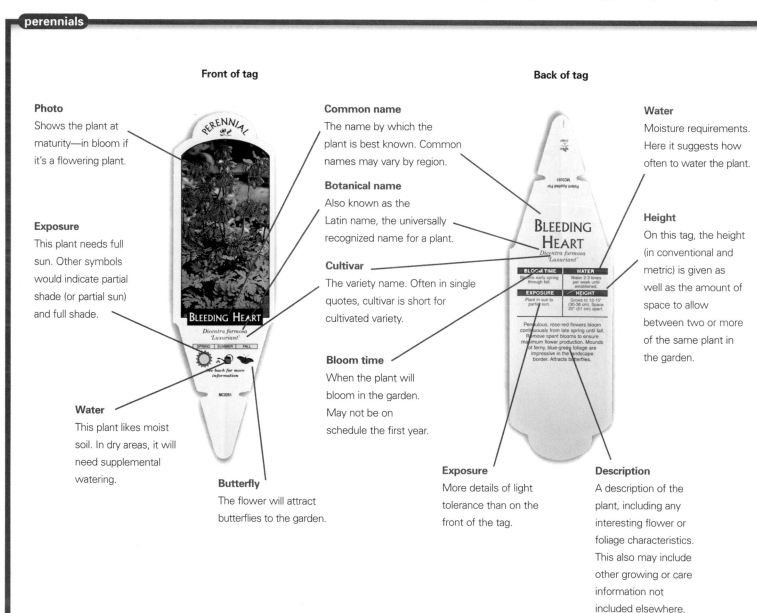

Front of tag

Back of tag

Photo
Shows the plant at maturity—in bloom if it's a flowering plant.

Exposure
This plant needs full sun. Other symbols would indicate partial shade (or partial sun) and full shade.

Water
This plant likes moist soil. In dry areas, it will need supplemental watering.

Butterfly
The flower will attract butterflies to the garden.

Common name
The name by which the plant is best known. Common names may vary by region.

Botanical name
Also known as the Latin name, the universally recognized name for a plant.

Cultivar
The variety name. Often in single quotes, cultivar is short for cultivated variety.

Bloom time
When the plant will bloom in the garden. May not be on schedule the first year.

Water
Moisture requirements. Here it suggests how often to water the plant.

Height
On this tag, the height (in conventional and metric) is given as well as the amount of space to allow between two or more of the same plant in the garden.

Exposure
More details of light tolerance than on the front of the tag.

Description
A description of the plant, including any interesting flower or foliage characteristics. This also may include other growing or care information not included elsewhere.

of the plant as well as a photo of the plant in bloom. ⁋Generally speaking, the front of the tag—the side with the color photo—is at-a-glance information. Often there are symbols (instead of words), indicating the light, soil, and/or moisture requirements. Unfortunately there isn't universal symbolism—except for a sun indicating that the plant requires more than six hours of sunlight per day—so you often need to turn to the back of the tag for more detailed information.

151

annuals

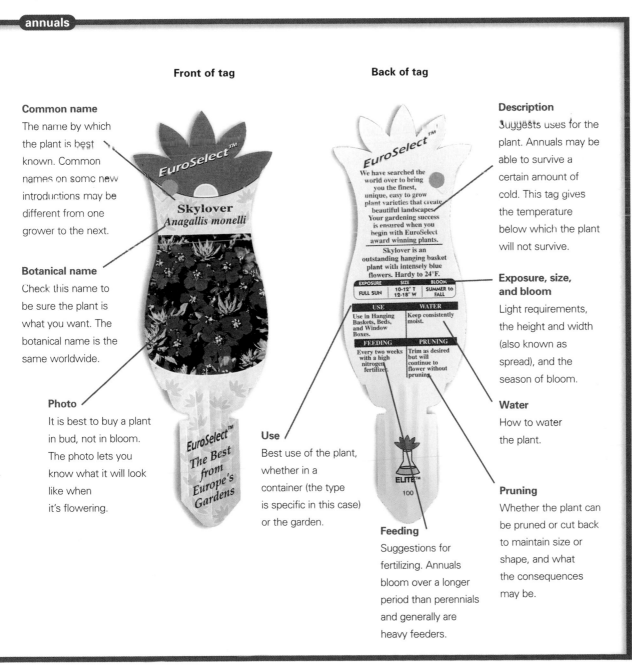

Front of tag

Back of tag

Common name
The name by which the plant is best known. Common names on some new introductions may be different from one grower to the next.

Botanical name
Check this name to be sure the plant is what you want. The botanical name is the same worldwide.

Photo
It is best to buy a plant in bud, not in bloom. The photo lets you know what it will look like when it's flowering.

Use
Best use of the plant, whether in a container (the type is specific in this case) or the garden.

Feeding
Suggestions for fertilizing. Annuals bloom over a longer period than perennials and generally are heavy feeders.

Description
Suggests uses for the plant. Annuals may be able to survive a certain amount of cold. This tag gives the temperature below which the plant will not survive.

Exposure, size, and bloom
Light requirements, the height and width (also known as spread), and the season of bloom.

Water
How to water the plant.

Pruning
Whether the plant can be pruned or cut back to maintain size or shape, and what the consequences may be.

digging a garden bed

Planning your approach ahead of time helps ensure that your new bed will be successful. There are several issues to consider before you actually put shovel to soil. Location is critical. Beds intended to display colorful flowers must receive at least 6 to 8 hours of sun a day. As a result, this type of bed usually replaces lawn, which means you'll have to remove grass or sod first. Beds that are anchored by large trees or shrubs receive much less light and require shade-loving plants. Dig here with great care to avoid damaging the many roots in the top 12 inches of soil. ▼Another issue is size. Even under the best circumstances, gardens are arduous to dig. Opt for a manageable project.

YOU WILL NEED

- stakes
- string
- garden spade
- organic matter, such as compost, well-rotted manure, or leaf mold
- shovel
- granular fertilizer
- steel (garden) rake

1 Lay out the shape of the garden bed with stakes and string to establish a pleasing shape and size. Slide a spade under the existing lawn to free it from the soil.

2 Add organic matter to the exposed soil to improve its texture, drainage, and moisture retention. Dig it into the top 10 inches. This is a good time to add granular, slow-acting fertilizer, too.

3 Rake the soil smooth, removing small stones and breaking up lumps of soil. Make the bed as level as possible to ensure even distribution of rainwater.

designing the bed

Garden beds may be any shape or size. Most often they're borders, backed by a fence, wall, walkway, or building foundation. These beds are viewed from the front, so locate the tallest plants near the back, where they won't block the view of smaller ones. Plants of medium height go in the middle, and the shortest ones are at the front. Island beds typically sit in the middle of an expanse of lawn, so you and everyone else can view them from all sides. In this case, place the tallest plants at the center of the bed. Put medium ones around them, and reserve the shortest for the perimeter of the bed.

Initially the width of a border bed might be double your arm's reach. Island beds can be twice that, because they're reachable from two sides. Remember that it's relatively easy to enlarge a bed later. Keep the bed in proportion to its surroundings. A bed along a wall should not be wider than the wall is tall. A bed under one or more trees or shrubs should be at least as wide as the height of the trees. ❧Finally, consider the soil. Dig in organic matter to correct compaction and improve texture and fertility. In areas where clay soil is unredeemable, consider raised beds to ensure good drainage.

weather

The cooler weather in fall is the best time to dig a new bed. It's also the ideal season to plant many perennials, shrubs, and trees. They have several months to establish strong roots before showtime in spring. After you dig and plant the bed, cover the exposed soil with a protective layer of chopped leaves or other mulch.

153

composting

When you make compost, you simply encourage the same decomposition process that takes place automatically in nature. All you need is yard and garden waste, moisture, and good air circulation to create a favorable environment for teeming populations of microscopic fungi, bacteria, and other organisms that live on plant surfaces. They break down the collected materials as they eat and reproduce in an elaborate food chain that gradually produces crumbly, black matter with a nearly neutral pH—"black gold" to gardeners. ❚Decide how quickly you want compost. The passive system is slower but easier. As yard wastes accumulate over the months, pile them in a heap in a back part of

YOU WILL NEED

- cart or wheelbarrow
- composting fork
- brown/dry organic material (carbon)
- green organic material (nitrogen)
- water
- lime, fertilizer, topsoil, compost activator (optional)
- compost thermometer (optional)

building the pile

1 Build an active compost pile by mixing yard and nonmeat kitchen waste in a loose heap that is roughly 3' × 3' × 3'. The smaller the pieces, the faster the microbial activity will decompose them.

2 Be sure there's much more brown (carbon-based) than green (nitrogen-based) material to spur the decomposition process. Lime, fertilizer, topsoil, and activators are optional additives.

3 If the materials aren't already moist, dampen them before you build the pile. There's no need to cover the pile—it won't smell. And rain is good for it.

4 Give the microbes new food and oxygen by turning the pile when the temperature drops. Compost is ready when it's dark and crumbly.

your property. After a year, dig underneath the pile to harvest a few bushels of compost. Keep adding to the pile and harvesting over time. Enclose the pile if it's an eyesore. In an active system—quicker but more physically demanding—you accelerate microbial action. Shred or chop moist materials into small pieces, then build the pile all at once. Check for heat in the core, indicating strong microbial activity. When the pile cools somewhat, turn it to add air and reinvigorate the microbes. Protect the pile from heavy rains, and add worms to speed the breakdown. Expect compost in six to 10 weeks.

don't compost wood

Separate sticks, twigs, pinecones, and other thick, woody items from the other raw materials before you build a compost pile. Because wood takes a long time to decompose, these items will cause lumps in the finished compost. An alternative is to chop or chip them into smaller pieces, then toss them in with the other materials.

155

kinds of compost containers

Use a triple-bin arrangement if you want to produce quantities of compost on a continuing basis. Removable front slats help you turn one pile into the next bin. Fill the first with new material.

You rotate these drum-type bins to turn the pile and provide more air to fuel decomposition. Turn the drum opening downward to empty the compost into a garden cart positioned under it.

Enclose unsightly passive piles that take years to decompose. Use wattle fencing, wire circles, or other materials that allow airflow.

Finished compost—"black gold"—is dark and crumbly. The original raw materials are no longer recognizable except for occasional twigs.

ornamenting the garden

Ornaments are the finishing touches to a garden. They personalize the space, making it truly yours. In their main role as decorative objects, they can add elements of color, shape, texture, and whimsy—all reflecting the interests and personality of you, the owner. ❧Your garden is a wonderful venue to display art of all kinds. If you choose ornaments with design features that reflect bygone eras, they'll evoke nostalgia. You can use ornaments to carry out period themes such as a Victorian garden or a French estate garden. Urns, gates, fences, sculpture, fountains, old tools, and artifacts punctuate the overall effect of your garden—sometimes with a period, sometimes with an

weather

In regions with cold winters, outdoor ornaments have to stand up to alternating freezing and thawing over several months. Unless they're made of wood, concrete, metal, or other frost-proof materials, they'll crack. When in doubt, move them indoors before the first frost. For sure, bring in ceramic or terra-cotta plaques, figurines, and containers.

Ornaments with animal motifs are popular in gardens. If you're a fan of frogs, owls, snakes, rabbits, or other animals, you can have fun displaying your collection throughout the landscape.

Informal art pieces, such as this Southwestern-style metal sculpture, work well in open meadow gardens and lawn areas. They're especially effective when grouped and viewed from a distance.

Sculptures of wildlife enhance a natural-looking garden. These ducks blend with the rocks and add a suggestion of movement at the edge of the pond.

Objects that reflect light are welcome additions to gardens. Gazing balls and birdbaths brighten shaded spots and add perspective.

exclamation point. ❧Garden ornaments can be practical, too. They're useful in establishing focal points to guide the eye toward an intersection of paths or to a vista. As accents, they draw notice to a nook, a special plant, or steps. Decorative bridges, stepping-stones, and lights direct foot traffic.

Distinctive furniture invites visitors to rest and reflect in the garden. Matched objects, used repetitively, reinforce a sense of balance and symmetry in a formal design. Other ornaments, such as sundials and weather vanes, provide practical information for those inclined to notice.

Birdhouses are decorative and functional, whether they are mounted or hung. Those with proper-sized holes and ventilation attract feathered friends to patrol your garden for insect pests.

Humor is important, too. Here the colorful menagerie adds an element of surprise and delight because these animals are foreign to this environment.

Add fun and whimsy to a garden by tucking a bashful figure under foliage where mythical gnomes are said to hide.

ornamenting the garden (cont'd.)

Ornaments also contribute to the life and health of your garden. Birdhouses, bird feeders, birdbaths, fountains, and toad shelters invite and protect wildlife that add sound and movement to the scene and help control insect pests, as well. Structural ornaments such as arbors, tuteurs, gazebos, and pergolas, support plants, helping define spaces and boundries. ❦Every garden has a special character and feeling. Use ornaments that have pleasing color, good proportion, and unique design. There are no rules for garden art, except possibly to avoid overdoing it. But even that's OK if the spirit moves you.

round and round

Orbs and spheres are enjoying renewed popularity as garden accessories. Gazing balls, concrete or marble balls, crafted willow-branch spheres, round paper lanterns, and colorful plastic bubbles have many uses in the landscape. Hang them from trees, float them on water, or wrap them in lights to evoke the music of the planets.

❦For the best effect, integrate ornaments and plants. Daisies floating in this birdbath seem to emphasize the interdependence of the flowers, the moisture, and the creatures who visit both.

❦A pedestal provides vertical interest. Topped with a round object—armillary sphere, gazing ball, or sundial—it suggests a flower on a stem. Its inanimate features contrast with the living plants nearby.

❦Achieve a special effect by using familiar ornaments in new ways. This gazing ball nestled among the plants at ground level surprises passersby when they notice its reflections in the sun.

❦Collectors enjoy displaying their treasures in the garden. Some collectibles, such as these watering cans, are already at home there. Anything that can endure weather is a potential garden ornament.

The presence of cherubs, fairies, and mythical figures endows a garden with a spiritual dimension.

Placement of ornaments enhances their effect. Here a swan glides on a lake of grape hyacinths.

Natural materials such as wood, stone, and clay harmonize well with any natural setting.

Ornaments borrowed from England, such as this staddle stone, pay homage to their source.

your garden plan

Use this space to draw in your garden

Sketch the garden as it exists now, or as you want it to be. You can include the house, walkways, and other structures, if you want, for an overview. You can draw the garden to whatever scale works best — one square equals 1 foot is the most common. Once the garden is drawn, you can use tracing paper over the drawing to see how new garden beds will work, before you start to dig.

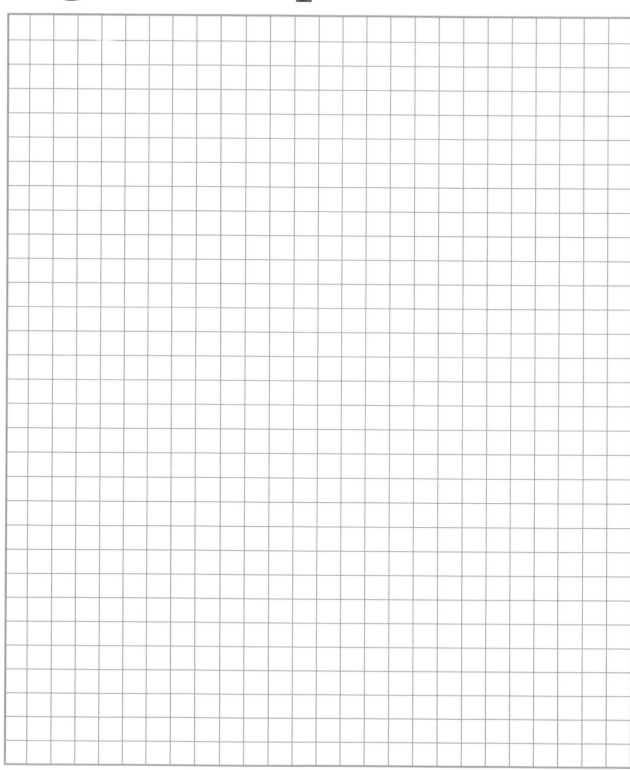

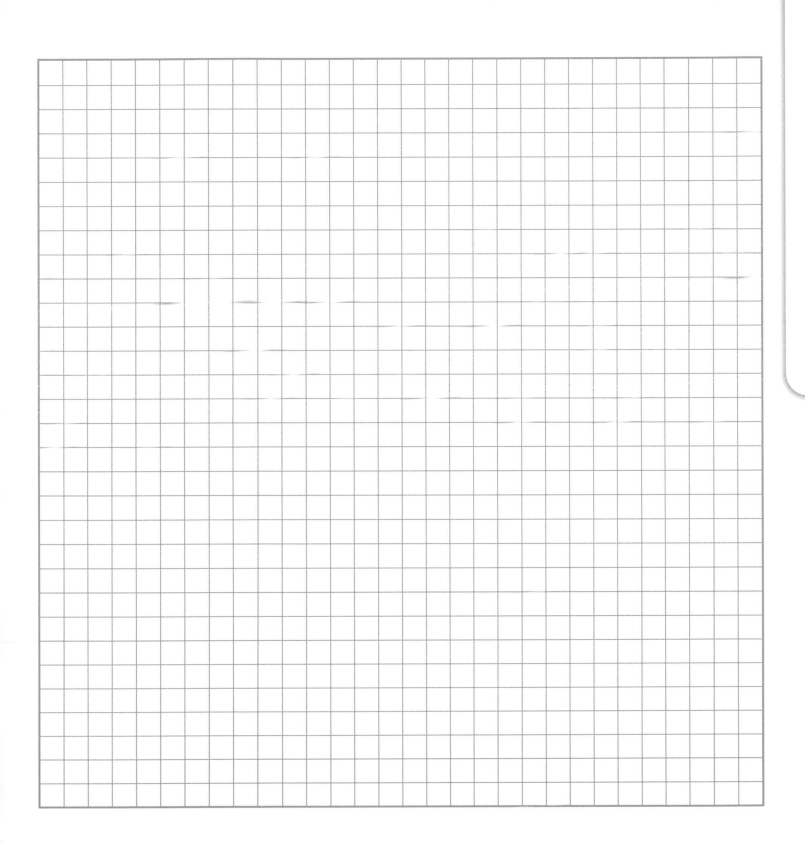

your plants

It's a good idea to keep track of the plants in your garden—

to help you remember what's planted where. Photocopy this and the following page, if you wish, to start a garden journal. Here you can keep records of each plant you buy: its name, the date when you planted it, and its location. The comments column is for any other information you want to remember, such as where you bought it, the date it bloomed, how long it stayed in bloom, the color of the flower, and any pest or disease problems. You'll find that this type of record keeping is helpful as your garden matures, allowing you to remember all its pertinent facts and history. Some people also record when (if) a plant dies, and why.

plant name	date planted	location

comments

plant sources

Mail-Order Nurseries and Seed Suppliers

key

(B) bulbs

(P) perennials

(S) seeds

Antique Rose Emporium (P) $5.00
9300 Lueckemeyer Rd.
Brenam, TX 77833–6453
800/441-0002

Brent & Becky's Bulbs (B) $1.00
7463 Heath Trail
Gloucester, VA 23061
804/693-3966

Burpee (S) free
300 Park Ave.
Warminster, PA 18991–0001
800/487-5530

The Cook's Garden (S) free
P.O. Box 535
Londonderry, VT 05148
800/457-9703

Forestfarm (P) $4.00
990 Tetherow Rd.
Williams, OR 97544-9599
541/846-7269

The Gourmet Gardener (S) free
8650 College Blvd.
Overland Park, KS 66210
913/345-0490

Heronswood Nursery Ltd. (P) $4.00
7530 NE 288th St.
Kingston, WA 98346
360/297-4172

Jackson & Perkins Co. (P) free
P.O. Box 1028
Medford, OR 97501
800/292-4769

J. L. Hudson, Seedsman (S) $1.00
Star Rte. 2, Box 337
La Honda, CA 94020
No phone

Johnny's Selected Seeds (S) free
Foss Hill Rd.
Albion, ME 04910–9731
207/437-4301

Kurt Bluemel, Inc. (P) $3.00
2740 Greene Ln.
Baldwin, MD 21013–9523
800/248-7584

Louisiana Nursery (P) $5.00
Rte. 7, Box 43
Opelousas, LA 70570
318/948-3696

McClure & Zimmerman (B) free
P.O. Box 368
Friesland, WI 53935-0368
800-883-6998

Niche Gardens (P) $3.00
1111 Dawson Rd.
Chapel Hill, NC 27516
919/967-0078

chapter six

Nichols Garden Nursery (S) free
1190 N. Pacific Hwy.
Albany, OR 97321–9599
541/846-7269

Park Seed Company (S) free
One Parkton Ave.
Greenwood, SC 29647–0001
800/845-3369

Pinetree Garden Seeds (S) free
Box 300
New Gloucester, ME 04260
207/926-3400

Plant Delights Nursery (P) $2.00
9241 Sauls Rd.
Raleigh, NC 27603
919/772-4794

Richters (S)
Goodwood
Ontario L0C 1A0 Canada
905/640-6677

Roses of Yesterday (P) $3.00
802 Brown's Valley Rd.
Watsonville, CA 95076–0398
408/724-3537

Seed Savers Exchange (S) free
3076 North Winn Rd.
Decorah, IA 52101
319/382-5990

Select Seed (S) $3.00
81 Stickney Hill Rd.
Union, CT 06076-4617
203/684-9310

Thompson & Morgan Inc. (S) free
P.O. Box 1308
Jackson, NJ 08527-0308
800/274-7333

Tranquil Lake Nursery (P) $1.00
45 River St.
Rehoboth, MA 02769–1395
508/252-4002

White Flower Farm (P) free
P.O. Box 50
Litchfield, CT 06759–0050
800/503-9624

Woodlanders (P) $2.00
1128 Colleton Ave.
Aiken, SC 29801
803/648-7522

Plants from the Internet
http://www.bhglive.com
http://www.garden.com
http://www.landscapeusa.com
http://www.vg.com

index

index